Dangerous Journeys

Other Piccolo True Adventures

Aidan Chambers
Haunted Houses
More Haunted Houses
Great British Ghosts
Great Ghosts of the World

Richard Garrett
They Must Have Been Crazy
Hoaxes and Swindles
True Tales of Detection
Narrow Squeaks!
Great Sea Mysteries

John Gilbert
Highwaymen and Outlaws
Pirates and Buccaneers

Frank Hatherley
Bushrangers Bold!

Marie Herbert
Great Polar Adventures

George Laycock
Strange Monsters and Great Searches

Carey Miller
Submarines!
Airships and Balloons
Baffling Mysteries

Nicholas Monsarrat
The Boys' Book of the Sea

Sorche Nic Leodhas
Scottish Ghosts

Piccolo True Adventures

Richard Garrett

DANGEROUS JOURNEYS

text illustrations by Gary Rees
cover illustration by Edward Mortelmans

Piccolo Original
Pan Books London and Sydney

First published 1978 by Pan Books Ltd,
Cavaye Place, London SW10 9PG
© Richard Garrett 1978
ISBN 0 330 25346 8
Printed and bound in Great Britain by
Cox & Wyman Ltd, London, Reading and Fakenham

'Second to the right,' said Peter,
'and then straight on till morning.'

J. M. Barrie –
Peter Pan's directions on how to reach the Neverland

Contents

Introduction

When people come to a range of mountains they react in different ways. Some get out their cameras, take pictures, say, 'Isn't it pretty', and turn away. Others become filled with a kind of longing. They want to discover what lies on the far side. To them the mountains represent a wall that must be climbed.

This book is about such people – the explorers who risked their lives on journeys of discovery. Later on, in many cases, the settlers followed, and civilization (as they liked to call it) was brought to the darker corners of the earth.

Most of the regions were already inhabited. The natives were supposed to be grateful for the coming of the white man. He brought with him medicine and Christianity and machines and guns and all sorts of ideas and objects they had never heard about before.

Unfortunately a lot of things went wrong. If the white men had not also imported diseases there would have been no need for the medicines. The machines polluted an otherwise pure atmosphere; the guns taught them an art of warfare just as barbarous as their own; and the teaching of Christianity might have been more convincing if the fair-skinned strangers had practised as well as preached it.

One of the intruders' particularly puzzling customs was the idea of justice. If a man stole, he was harshly punished. Nobody could complain about that, as the natives themselves had similar views. But if a white man stuck a stick with a flag on it into a patch of ground, and said 'this is mine', or 'this is my country's', nobody grumbled. He might even have been called a hero.

Nobody paused to consider that this particular piece of earth might belong to a Red Indian, to a Zulu, to an Inca – that, by helping himself to it, the white man was stealing. There was, it seemed, one law for those who came to a place – and another for those who actually belonged to it.

Does this sound as if the explorers should have remained at home ? I hope not; for they showed us what a fascinating place the earth is. They were men of courage – whose adventures were extremely exciting. In trying to tell their stories I have wanted to pay tribute to them. It was those who came afterwards that made the mess.

R.G.
Tunbridge Wells

1 Find Livingstone!

The mystery intrigued and worried a great many people. The Queen herself was known to be anxious. For years she had taken a keen and admiring interest in the African exploits of Dr David Livingstone. Whenever a steamer docked in London from Zanzibar it carried a sack of his letters and reports. Even when he ran out of ink he improvised by using the juice of crushed berries. But now, for no apparent reason, there was silence. It was so unlike Livingstone that it seemed possible he was dead.

In 1868 a rumour which was printed in *The Times* suggested that he had been killed on the shore of Lake Nyasa. It would certainly have explained the lack of correspondence. Nevertheless, there were some who doubted it. The Royal Geographical Society set about organizing an expedition to discover the truth. Before it departed, however, another report reached London. The earlier story was a lie broadcast by African porters who had deserted the doctor. He was, in fact, alive and well. Indeed, shortly afterwards, a letter arrived from Livingstone himself.

But this was no more than a brief respite. Soon afterwards he vanished again. This time it seemed that he must be dead. The 1860s gave way to the 1870s, and still no word came.

David Livingstone had been born in Lanarkshire in 1813. After working in a cotton mill he had attended Glasgow University as a medical student. When he was qualified he joined the London Missionary Society. By the mid-1850s he was in the heart of Africa – and sending home the first of his long line of letters.

Livingstone was many men rolled into one. Explorer, doctor, preacher – there seemed no end to his talents. But most of all he was inspired by an ideal. The rich men of Africa were the Arab dealers who made fortunes out of slaves. According to Livingstone, there was only one way of ending this terrible traffic in humanity: to open up the continent to legitimate commerce and Christianity. Some people disagreed with him; some simply did not care. If he were dead it would certainly save the slave traders a good deal of trouble. There was nobody fit to take over the struggle that he had begun.

After Livingstone's second disappearance little attempt had been made to find him. Eventually it was an American who took up the challenge. He may have been inspired by the doctor's dream of an enlightened Africa; more likely he was anxious to sell newspapers. His name was James Gordon Bennett – European manager of the *New York Herald*. The man he chose for the assignment was his star reporter, Henry Morton Stanley.

Stanley was an illegitimate child who had been brought up in a Welsh workhouse. The man who ran the place was a sadist, and those cruel years of his early youth shaped his character. He was tough, resourceful, very ambitious and no less ruthless. As soon as he was able to leave the establishment he went to sea as a cabin boy. His original name was John Rowlands. Over in America, however, he was adopted by a kind-hearted merchant named Henry Morton Stanley. 'John Rowlands' was thrown away, and the young man assumed his benefactor's name.

He was now living the life of an adventurer. He served on both sides during the American Civil War, fought in the battles against the Red Indians, tried to make his fortune during the Californian gold rush, spent more time at sea and eventually became a newspaper man. By 1870 he had joined the *New York Herald* as a foreign correspondent.

On the morning of 16 October 1869 Stanley was in Madrid. He had just finished breakfast when he was handed a telegram. 'Come to Paris on important business,' it read. It was signed by James Gordon Bennett. Stanley packed his bags and caught the three p.m. train. On the following night he presented himself at Bennett's room in the Grand Hotel.

The newspaper magnate was in bed. As he slung a dressing gown over his shoulders he suddenly asked, 'Where do you think Livingstone is ?' Stanley replied that he had no idea. Bennett said that he felt sure the doctor was alive – and that he could be found. Stanley might make whatever plans he liked, and there was no limit to the number of dollars he could spend. 'But,' Bennett ordered in the voice of a man who was used to having his own way, 'find Livingstone.'

If that had been his only task it would have been problem enough. But Bennett had a few other matters that needed attention. Stanley was to visit Egypt to cover the opening of the Suez Canal; compile a guide book about the Lower Nile; report on excavations in Jerusalem; write a piece about the battlefields of the Crimean War; and send in other stories from as far away as Persia and India. Once he had dealt with these matters he could begin looking for the missing doctor. Despite the way in which Bennett had emphasized the words '*find Livingstone*', the assignment did not seem to be very urgent.

Stanley completed his other work in a surprisingly short time and arrived in Zanzibar on 6 January 1871. The British Consul, John Kirk, agreed that Livingstone *might* be alive. But, he explained, the doctor was a difficult man to deal with. He preferred to be on his own, and he doubted whether Stanley could expect much of a welcome if he found him. 'To tell you the truth,' Kirk said, 'I do not think he would like it very well.' Stanley found the interview depressing, and even considered giving up the attempt. But then Bennett's instructions came back to him, and he reflected that, 'I did not suppose, though I had so readily consented to search for the Doctor, that the path to Central Africa was strewn with roses.' A job was a job; he would have to get on with it.

He made his plans carefully. Assembling such evidence as he could find, he came to the conclusion that the most likely place to discover traces of Livingstone would be on the shore of Lake Tanganyika – possibly in the vicinity of a village named Ujiji. In a direct line it was about six hundred miles – but the way was through forest and jungle, over hills and across scorching salt plains. It was, he felt, possible to count on the cooperation of any Arabs he might meet. The attitude of the natives was less predictable.

The English population at Zanzibar had given Stanley a cool reception. Nobody displayed any eagerness to accompany him on his trip. Nevertheless, he needed at least two white assistants. In the end he settled for a Londoner named Shaw, who had just lost his job as third mate on an American ship. For his other companion he chose an individual named William Farquhar. He was a good navigator and had plenty of energy. Unfortunately it soon became plain that he was a heavy drinker. Neither he nor Shaw was ideal, but nobody else was available.

It was all very well to hope for assistance from natives along the route. They would, however, expect payment. Currency was useless unless it took the form of gold coins. Bales of material were known to be acceptable, and people were continually talking about beads. 'Beads for the natives' – it was a kind of cliché. Whether, in fact, they were so eager for this form of adornment seems to be doubtful. Throughout his long journey Stanley parted with plenty of cloth, but the demands on his stock of cheap jewellery were small.

Any transaction was preceded by bargaining. To judge by the dialogue quoted in Stanley's account of his expedition (*How I Found Livingstone*), he was a shrewd and stubborn negotiator. When you look at the figures, however, it becomes clear that the natives usually came off best. In one instance a local chief demanded a hundred bales of material. Stanley offered twenty; but when the ball of commerce had been bounced backwards and forwards a few times he paid eighty. In return for this substantial outlay he received the promise of a safe passage through this ruler's kingdom.

As a travelling companion Henry Morton Stanley was not the most easy of men. His attitude to the African soldiers and porters was simple: if in doubt, flog them. Attempts to desert were the most common offences. Sometimes the punishment was executed with a whip normally used to coax more effort out of the mules. Sometimes Stanley himself carried it out – using his cane. None of the native followers was exempt; even

Mbarak Bombay, his so-called 'captain of soldiers', had received a good many lashes by the time the journey was done.

One might have suspected that such angry brutality would produce a mutiny. Stanley, however, professed that the treatment brought on a mood of penitence. If he is to be believed, the victims saw some kind of logic in it, and the weals on their backs merely strengthened their loyalty to him. Possibly – but by the time the cavalcade reached its destination few of the original members were still in its ranks.

Quite early on, the two white assistants made it clear that they had suffered enough from Stanley's harsh tongue and the rigours of jungle travel. The trouble began at breakfast when Shaw looked at the freshly roasted goat and snarled: 'What dog's meat is this ?' He then said, 'It is a downright shame the way you treat us.' The row reached a climax when Stanley hit Shaw in the face and knocked him over. He then ordered Mbarak Bombay to take down the unfortunate fellow's tent, to seize his firearms, and to move all his other possessions to a point a couple of hundred yards outside the camp. If Shaw was dissatisfied with his treatment he could go home through the jungle – on his own.

Eventually common sense returned. Shaw apologized and Stanley forgave him. After that, however, the relationship between the two men never regained its earlier quality. In Stanley's diary, we read such testy comments as 'Shaw will not work. I cannot get him to stir himself,' and 'I am sure he is practising a trick on me . . . if I took a stick I could take the nonsense out of him,' and 'Shaw is a sentimental driveller.' During the early days of the trek the ex-merchant navy officer had enlivened the evenings by playing tunes on a cheap accordion. Now, one suspects, the accordion was silent.

None of them were well. Shaw suffered from an intermittent fever, and Farquhar became so ill that he had to be left behind. By the middle of August he was dead. Stanley himself succumbed to malaria on several occasions – despite copious doses of quinine. The bouts began with a feeling of lassitude which developed into drowsiness. Backache, shivering, a distortion of vision, and a throbbing in the temples followed. It was like a particularly severe attack of flu. Sometimes the sickness came and went in twelve hours. Once it lasted three weeks.

During this severe bout Stanley lost all idea of time. When he recovered there were seven days that, no matter how hard he tried, he could not account for. He had spent them in a state of delirium – reliving his past life. He endured again the horrors of life in the Welsh workhouse; he remembered the generous American merchant who had given him a new name and a new chance; and he fought once more the battles of the Civil War.

But presently the fever subsided and he returned to reality. It was just as well, for the expedition had now reached a place named Unyanyembe, and there were many problems to be faced.

The trouble was that the road (if it could be called one) that led to Ujiji had been cut. There was, it seemed, a war in progress. On the one hand, there were the Arabs who had established a trading post nearby at Tabora and, on the other, a young African king named Mirambo. Both sides wished to corner the territory's trade in ivory. The Arabs had more men and better weapons, but Mirambo was a more accomplished warrior.

He was a young man with long hair who, so Stanley was told, always held an umbrella over his head. Originally he had been a robber. As time went on, his ideas became more ambitious – until he achieved the monarchy of Uyoweh by the simplest possible method. When the reigning sovereign died, he sat down on the throne before anyone had a chance to consider who was the rightful heir.

According to Mirambo, he was fighting the Arabs because they would not support his campaign to overrun neighbouring countries. There may have been some truth in it; but, like most of these things, business was at the heart of the matter. Indeed, one of his first actions was to levy a toll for the route between Tabora and Ujiji. In return for the safe conduct of a caravan, he demanded five kegs of gunpowder, five guns, and five bales of cloth. The price was exorbitant – especially as the rifles and the gunpowder might well be used against the very merchants who had supplied them. Thereafter, the road was closed.

As a war it was a poor substitute for such elaborately staged conflicts as the Crimean, or even the British Abyssinian campaign (which had set ablaze the north-east corner of Africa in 1867). Most of the encounters were confused and indecisive; sometimes the action was confined to burning the long grass that concealed Mirambo's warriors. Stanley inevitably became involved; mainly because he needed to clear the way to Ujiji, but also because he wished to assist the Arabs. After all, they had treated him very well on the long trail that stretched back to Zanzibar.

It is perhaps strange that, in searching for Livingstone, Stanley should have allied himself to the very slave traders whose commerce the doctor was determined to end. But Africa was full of unlikely happenings. Some years later Stanley came face-to-face with Mirambo. Instead of the villain he had expected he met a handsome 35-year-old Negro without a touch of arrogance. He described him as 'a thorough African *gentleman*'.

What with attacks of fever and brief battles against Mirambo's warriors, the expedition was delayed at Unyanyembe for the better part of three months. Eventually the small war in the large continent came to an end when Mirambo's forces attacked a neighbouring village. Three of his key men were shot down by rifle fire. When he began to withdraw, the inhabitants ran out and gave chase. The robber king and his remaining troops were put to flight. The road to Ujiji was clear at last.

Stanley had lost a good deal of time. When he moved off, however, his health improved and he suffered no further attacks of fever. What was more, he had come across mail and provisions at Unyanyembe addressed to 'Dr Livingstone, Ujiji'. One of the packets of letters was dated '1 November 1870'. Without the supplies it was unlikely that the doctor had travelled any distance from his base. It was enough to hope that he was still alive.

Shaw, in Stanley's eyes, was becoming more and more tiresome. The truth, no doubt, was that he was not so robust as the tough American journalist. All the hardships and illnesses had worn him out. He was apt to fall off his horse, to lie on the ground beneath the blazing sun, or, unaccountably, to burst into tears. He needed help and sympathy. Stanley, with his harsh memories of life in the workhouse, was not the man to provide it. One afternoon in late September Stanley agreed that his unhappy companion should be sent back down the trail. That night, Shaw played his accordion for the last time. He finished the recital with 'Home, Sweet Home'. Next morning he was carried off on a litter. Somewhere along the road, he died.

November had shuffled on to the calendar before they approached Lake Tanganyika. On the third of that month they encountered a caravan of eighty men outward bound from Ujiji. The leader said that a white man had recently arrived in the village. He was an old man with a long white beard who had travelled a great distance. A week later, the 236th day since they had left the coast, they covered the last leg of the journey. It was, Stanley recalled, 'a happy, glorious morning. The air is fresh and cool. The sky lovingly smiles on the earth and her children.' The United States flag was flying bravely at the head of the column as, to their left, they saw the huge still waters of the lake – and, ahead of them, Ujiji.

Stanley ordered the rifles to be loaded and a ragged salute punctured the quiet of the morning. The people of Ujiji came out to meet them, and Stanley heard a quiet voice say, 'Good morning, sir.' The speaker explained that he was 'Susi, the servant of Dr Livingstone'. Where was the doctor? In the village. Could he be sure? Certainly, he had been with him a few moments ago. Wrote Stanley:

What would I not have given for a bit of friendly wilderness, where, unseen, I might vent my joy in some mad freak, such as idiotically biting my hand, turning a somersault, or slashing at trees, in order to allay those exciting feelings that are well nigh uncontrollable. My heart beats fast, but I must not let my face betray my

emotions, lest it shall detract from the dignity of a white man appearing under such extraordinary circumstances.

He advanced towards the village. There, standing in front of a semi-circle of Arabs, was a white man with a grey beard. He was wearing a blue cap with a gold band round it; a red waistcoat and grey tweed trousers. Stanley took off his cap, and said:

'Dr Livingstone, I presume ?'

The old man smiled and raised his cap. 'Yes,' he said.

Contrary to the opinion of the English consul at Zanzibar, Dr Livingstone was pleased to see Stanley, and he was very grateful for the supplies he brought. If he had been left on his own for much longer he would have been reduced to begging off the very Arabs whose slave-trading activities he had tried to abolish. Stanley was so impressed by him that, when Livingstone died three years later, he tried to carry on the missionary's work. In 1878 he founded the Congo Free State with King Leopold of the Belgiums. Among his many honours was a British knighthood. He died in 1904.

2 The Forbidden City

During a June day in 1812 a travel-stained figure called at the Calcutta offices of the East India Company. He had a long, pointed beard and he was dressed in tattered Chinese robes. When an official asked what he wanted, he replied in perfect English that he had just returned from Lhasa. The company's manager, who must have been a very dull character, refused to be impressed. If that was all, he said, why was he wasting his time?

Thomas Manning (for that was the man's name) deserved a better reception. He had just accomplished what no European had ever done before: *he had been to the forbidden city*. Some years earlier two Englishmen had journeyed to Tibet, but they had not been able to enter Lhasa. Perched on the roof of the world, ringed by huge mountains, and governed by men who hated foreigners, this city was out-of-bounds.

But, somehow, Manning had penetrated the barrier. Other people would have been proud of such an achievement. On the whole, however, he was disappointed. Lhasa had not been his objective at all. If everything had gone according to plan it would have been a staging post on a much longer trip. What he really wanted was to visit Peking. It was, admittedly, a roundabout way of getting there: but he could see no other.

Tibet occupies a plateau 3,658 metres above sea level. It is walled in by the Himalayas to the south and by the

Kunlun Mountains in the north. To reach it was a daunting task for even the most intrepid explorer with plenty of money and equipment behind him. But there was nothing particularly brave about Thomas Manning, and nor were there large sums of cash to finance the trip. He set off casually and with no experience of such exploits. Apart from taking an interpreter and a few gifts to amuse the natives, he might have been departing for a Sunday afternoon's stroll in the park.

Thomas Manning was born in 1772, the son of a Norfolk clergyman. Despite a reasonably distinguished career at Cambridge, he left the university without taking a degree. For the next few years he worked as a tutor in the town – teaching mathematics and writing a book on arithmetic and algebra. But Manning was becoming interested in Chinese. Having studied the language, he decided that the only way to improve his knowledge was to visit China. In 1806 he secured a job with the East India Company, and sailed from London in the *Thames*. After a long and not very comfortable voyage he landed at Canton.

Whatever ideas he may have had about journeying onwards to Peking were quickly crushed. The Chinese regarded the Europeans as hangers-on. They were, perhaps, necessary – but they were not particularly welcome. When he applied to the authorities for a pass to the interior he was brusquely refused. He became angry but the official was unrelenting. The way was closed; he would have to find some other route. The only possibility, he presently decided, was to climb over the top of India and travel via Tibet. It was rather like going from London to Edinburgh by way of Cardiff, but the end was enough to justify the apparently strange means.

A portrait of Manning shows a good-looking, rather
serious young man. In fact, the portrait is deceptive. He
was inclined to make rather bad jokes. He laughed easily
and often; and, when he persuaded the East India
Company to transfer him to Calcutta, he began to indulge
in eccentricities. He grew a beard, which was
unfashionable at the time, and replaced his European
clothes by what he described as 'the robes of a Tartar
gentleman'. Significantly, the only Chinese book he
translated was a collection of funny stories. The East
India Company officials were not amused by an
employee who, in their opinion, was obviously going out
of his mind. Other people thought he was fun.

Before very long Thomas Manning had become a
minor celebrity. It may have been gratifying to his pride,
but it did nothing to help him along the road to Peking.
When he suggested the Company should commission
him to manage its interests in Tibet, the governor refused.
Since all business stopped at the Indian frontier it was,
perhaps, understandable. Nevertheless, this stronghold
of British overseas trade had backed George Bogle and
Samuel Turner – the two men who had crossed the
Himalayas some years earlier. To have shown a little
interest would, to say the least, have been friendly.

Nothing daunted, Manning decided to go it alone.
Accompanied only by a Chinaman from Macao – whom
he sometimes referred to as his servant and sometimes as
his interpreter, but whom he never mentioned by name –
he set off for the mountains. Much of the journey was on
horseback. For many people, this would have been
agreeable, but Manning did not sit easily in the saddle.
Sometimes he fell off; at the best of times he and the
beast found it hard to conceal their mutual dislike. His

relationship with human beings was, on the whole, better. None of them suspected that he was an Englishman; several assumed he was a Moslem – but to most, he was that rare and enigmatic figure, a mysterious stranger.

Before setting out for the East he had attended a quick course in medicine at the Westminster Hospital in London. It was too short to be of much value; even by the poor standards of the day he was far from expert. Nevertheless, he was full of confidence and this may have helped to build his reputation as a healer. Wherever he halted for the night patients came to see him. His remedies consisted of opium (which dulled the pain but cured nothing), antimony (a poison that is not used nowadays), and a concoction with the fearsome name of 'Fowler's Solution of Arsenic'. He considered himself especially good at treating coughs, stomach complaints, and eye infections. If his medicine chest is anything to go by, it seems surprising that anyone survived.

The journey from India into Tibet was not especially dramatic. On either side of the route there were giant mountains such as Everest, but he followed reasonably well-worn tracks. On one occasion he had to wade through a torrent with ice-cold water raging about him. On another, when they were approaching the top of a 3,500 metre ridge, he and his Chinese companion had to sleep out on the mountainside. In Bhutan, he was held captive for three weeks in a guardroom. But, for most of the time, he slept under cover and the people were friendly. Now and then he handed out gifts – mostly small sums of money and mirrors – to minor officials. But it was his role of doctor that won him the most popularity. People felt better after they had been to see him – no doubt because he dosed them heavily with opium.

When, after an unusually hard day, his servant's skin began to peel off, this unhappy man sought Manning's advice. He received little sympathy – and no remedy. 'I told him it would do him good,' Manning wrote in his diary, 'and prevent fever.' Strangely enough, the reassurance seems to have worked. At any rate there were no more complaints from the ailing Chinaman.

They crossed into Tibet without any difficulty. But now they had to obtain a permit to visit Lhasa. It was not easy. As a European Manning would certainly have been turned back; but nobody, so far, had penetrated his disguise.

Lhasa is situated in the southern half of the largest plateau in the world. The temperature is mostly extremely cold – though, during the brief summer, it can be pleasantly warm. There are few trees, the grass is stunted, it is bleak and barren – a rock-strewn world of desolation.

But not only is Lhasa the world's highest city, it is also probably the most sacred. Until recently it was the home of the Dalai Lama – the fabulous monk who, according to believers, is an incarnation of Buddha. Until 1720 the Dalai Lama had been the ruler of Tibet. In that year the Chinese occupied it, and they controlled the country until 1912. In 1950, when they returned, the Dalai Lama fled to India, and Communism did its best to oust Buddhism as the people's faith.

When Manning was in Tibet, the Chinese officials were still anxious to halt the footsteps of inquisitive foreigners – even wandering doctors clad in Tartar robes. However, shortly after crossing the frontier, he received a rare piece of luck. He was staying at a town named Phari when suddenly he was turned out of his quarters. Apparently they were needed to accommodate a visiting Chinese general and his staff. Protesting loudly, Manning moved into poorer lodgings that were cold and dirty and infested with rats. However, this eccentric 39-year-old Englishman was not one to harbour grudges. When the general arrived he called on him and presented him with two bottles of cherry brandy and a wine glass. Thereafter the two men became great friends. The general promised to support Manning's application for a permit. Indeed, he did more: he offered to escort him to Lhasa.

Just before dawn on 5 November 1811 a gun was fired and the party set off. They travelled slowly, sometimes covering only ten miles in a day, sometimes thirty. It depended on the general's mood. The going was bitterly cold. At night they huddled around fires, eating rice and mutton and doubtless washing it down with cherry brandy. When they reached a town named Gyantse the general became critical of Manning's appearance. The beard, he said, was splendid; a magnificent adornment for the chin. He doubted whether, in all his lifetime of soldiering, he'd ever seen a finer example. The Tartar robes, on the other hand, were less satisfactory. Not only did they look wrong; they were not warm enough. He would do well to throw them away and buy a Chinese outfit. Manning agreed.

So far as we can tell, the general only once became angry with his companion. Their argument concerned horses. Manning had been given an uncommonly energetic steed to ride that day. Not surprisingly, it proved too much for him. After an hour or so of mutual

hatred the wretched animal bolted. It was eventually
halted by a cattle drover, but the general wanted to know
why his host had refused offers of a more docile mount.
Such stubbornness was unbecoming.

As they neared Lhasa, disturbing news reached
Manning. The Chinese occupying power was
represented by mandarins. By a horrible coincidence the
chief of these was the very official who, in Canton, had
turned down his plea to visit Peking. Memories of the
row they'd had were still vivid. Now, with a reunion
inevitable, it seemed probable that Manning would be
thrown into the city's deepest dungeon. Even the general
had misgivings. As they approached this citadel of faith,
where the devout can reach out and touch heaven, he
insisted they should separate. He did not wish their
friendliness to be taken the wrong way. In other words,
if Manning was arrested, he did not want to be regarded
as an accessory.

There had been no need for alarm. Manning took the
precaution of buying a pair of spectacles – which, he told
himself, would sufficiently disguise him. In fact, the
mandarin turned out to be so short-sighted that he could
not see far beyond his own pug-like nose. The new
arrival was just a vague shape such as one sees on a very
foggy day. He murmured a polite greeting, hoped
Manning had had a pleasant journey, and dismissed him
with a wave of his imperious hand.

Next came a meeting with the Dalai Lama. When
Manning had first glimpsed Lhasa it had seemed like a
town in a fairy tale – a place of perfect proportions, of
spotless whiteness that shone in the sunshine of a fine
afternoon. On closer inspection, however, it was
disappointing. The streets were mean and dirty and

infested with stray dogs; most of the houses were
scarcely more than hovels. However, above this
ramshackle assembly of squalor, the Dalai Lama's
palace stood high on a rock; a building that, in itself,
seemed to resemble a mountain capped with gilded
domes. It was almost, he observed, as if it *grew* out of
the hill.

To prepare himself for the encounter he had assembled
an odd assortment of gifts. It included a pair of brass
candlesticks that rightfully belonged to the East India
Company, a length of English cloth, a packet of Nanking
tea, and a bottle of lavender water.

Manning had hoped to ride up to the palace entrance,
but this was obviously impossible. The route lay up four
hundred steps that had been carved into the hillside.
Sweating and sometimes cursing he struggled upwards,
followed by his servant/interpreter who was carrying the
presents. Both men were nervous about the meeting.
Manning was not sure how to conduct himself; the
servant was in awe of a being who, according to his faith,
was only a small distance removed from God.

They were ushered through halls of unparalleled
magnificence until, at last, they reached the Dalai
Lama's room. What had they expected to find? A man
who was more than a man; a being of such power and
wisdom that all others seemed as pygmies? The Dalai
Lama, the supreme incarnation of the Buddhist faith,
turned out to be a cheerful-faced boy aged seven. Manning
went on his knees and touched the ground with his head
three times – then, for good measure, he did it a fourth
time in honour of the Regent who stood nearby. The
gifts were handed over. Somebody dropped the bottle of
lavender water which smashed to pieces on the floor. The

Dalai Lama asked a few polite questions, smiled nicely, and the audience was over.

Manning proceeded to set himself up as a doctor. There were plenty of patients, some of whom seemed to have nothing wrong with them. When the ailments were simple he brought relief. In more complicated cases he was less successful. One of his failures was the Dalai Lama's own physician. He was complaining of a stiff neck, a sore back, and a general weakness of mind and body. Manning put a plaster on his neck, dosed him with castor oil, and advised him to drink a little wine each day. It was obviously not the right treatment, for the man died shortly afterwards.

He referred to the ruling mandarins by code names. There was the Tartar Mandarin, who was his old enemy from Canton, and the Mad Mandarin, who was, well, mad. It might have been better if he had left the latter alone, but Doctor Manning overruled Explorer Manning by deciding that his lunacy could be cured. He was, of course, wrong. What was more, during his more frenzied moments, the patient babbled about a plot in which Tartar Mandarin had wrongfully put a man to death, and how they had both accepted bribes.

This was the first hint of trouble. The Tartar Mandarin heard about the activities of this amateur psychologist and, if the servant/interpreter was to be believed, proposed to interrogate him by torture. Manning himself acted tactlessly when he visited the temple. As a staunch Christian he refused to take part in such pagan rituals as twirling prayer wheels. The Buddhists resented it. To make matters worse, an unusually bright comet had appeared over Tibet. The ruling power decided that it was a warning against the mysterious doctor who had come among them.

It was now out of the question to hope for a permit to travel on to Peking. The only prudent course was to get out of Tibet as quickly as possible and back to the security of India. The authorities agreed to let him go, but the interpreter/servant was ordered to stay behind. Nobody knows what happened to him – though he was lucky if he escaped with his life.

And that is how, one day in the spring of 1812, a bedraggled individual, with a long beard and travel-torn Chinese clothing, turned up in Calcutta. Nobody seemed to be impressed by the news that he was the first European ever to visit Lhasa. Nobody heaped honours upon him, or gave him the fame he deserved. However, he did reach Peking in the end. He was appointed interpreter to the British Ambassador in China, Lord Amherst. Before accepting him, his lordship made one condition. Manning might keep his beard – but, in future, he must wear European clothes.

3 The Road to Timbuktu

Major Alexander Gordon Laing of the Royal African Colonial Corps was determined to visit the African town of Timbuktu. There were all sorts of reasons for his ambition. As an experienced explorer (his articles in the *Quarterly Journal of Science* had been well received), he wished to find out more about the River Niger – such as where, precisely, it poured itself out into the Atlantic. There was, too, the question of money. An organization dedicated to discovering Africa's interior had offered £3,000 to the first European who went there. What was more, Major Laing considered himself overdue for promotion. There was, he felt, the possibility that such a feat might attract the Army's attention. It would, surely, show him as a man who deserved higher rank.

And there was the challenge contained in the very name of Timbuktu. To the average Englishman, nowhere on earth seemed to be more remote. On the other hand, it was believed to be prosperous – a place where caravans crossing the desert converged; a capital city where they sold salt and slaves, ivory and gold.

It was something that appealed to the imagination. Other people had tried to get there – and they had failed. Many of them had died in the attempt. It was not surprising. The only road to Timbuktu lay across the Sahara Desert.

There is no larger desert in the world. It stretches 1,600 kilometres from the River Nile in the east to the

Atlantic Ocean in the west. To the north, it is not far removed from the Mediterranean; southwards, it burns itself out in the Niger's swamps. According to one calculation, it is as big as the USA.

Large areas of it are like an ocean: flat, the surface broken by ripples, a sea of sand that overlaps the horizon. Elsewhere it is a jumble of huge rocks and, in the centre, the ground rises to heights of over 2,700 metres.

It seems surprising that anyone or anything can exist in this most dreadful place, where the sun seems so angry and the sand is thirsty. At the beginning of the nineteenth century the inhabitants were strange, inward-looking men, who concealed their faces behind veils. They were intensely jealous of their world, and were fanatical in their Moslem faith. Intruders were not welcome. If the sun spared them and they found water to drink, the tribesmen were likely to murder them. To beat the desert was not enough. You had also to defeat its inhabitants.

Such, then, was the way to Timbuktu. An intelligent young officer like Major Laing was obviously aware of its perils. Did he, on the other hand, underrate them? For example, most Europeans who strayed into this scorching wilderness took the precaution of disguising themselves as Arabs. There were dangers enough, without drawing attention to themselves. Major Laing was less prudent. He went as he was – a European from the top of his sun helmet to the soles of his well-made boots. There was, perhaps, an arrogance about him. If so, it was foolish. The desert dictated the terms for a safe journey. One of them was humility.

Alexander Gordon Laing had been born in Edinburgh on 27 December 1793. His father ran a school in which, when he was only fifteen, he became a teacher. He joined the army when he was seventeen. He was certainly a romantic, but he was also an intellectual. His brother officers considered him clever – but, they had to admit, a trifle conceited. Perhaps he was, but Gordon Laing was less sure of himself than his manner suggested. He was apt to believe that other people (especially the high command at the War Office) were trying to do him down.

In the early spring of 1825, he arrived in Tripoli and presented himself at the home of the British Consul, Hamner Warrington. The Colonial Office had agreed to support his attempt to reach Timbuktu; Warrington was to give him every assistance. While the consul was doing his best to enlist help from the ruler of Tripoli, an indolent character known as the Bashaw, Laing suddenly found himself in an unfamiliar situation. At the age of thirty-one he had fallen in love. The object of his devotion was Emma Warrington, the consul's daughter. Much to his delight she obviously returned his affection. After nine weeks of courtship she agreed to marry him.

Warrington liked the young man. In letters to his chief in London he referred to his 'extreme gentlemanly manners' and to his 'honourable conduct'. Once he called him 'an old friend'. This was all very well when Laing was simply an army officer who hoped to cross the Sahara. When he became a prospective son-in-law, however, he was less satisfactory. He belonged to an unfashionable regiment, he was far from wealthy, and his family tree could be studied in detail without revealing any aristocratic connections. In a nutshell, Hamner Warrington had hoped his daughter would do better for herself.

Argument was useless: the young lady had made up

her mind. Since there was no clergyman in Tripoli, one of the consul's duties was to perform marriage ceremonies. Not only did Warrington have to agree to the match between Emma and Laing, but he had also to solemnize it. However, he insisted that it must eventually receive the blessing of a Church of England priest. Two days later Gordon Laing set off for the desert.

He had a small personal staff of three men. The Bashaw had arranged for him to be accompanied (and protected) by a sheik named Babani. The best that could be said of Babani was that he knew which way to go, and that he made sure the small caravan* never lacked food or water. In all other matters, one suspects, he was an above average rogue.

When the cavalcade reached its first oasis, a town named Ghadames, Laing discovered that his scientific instruments had all been broken, and a camel had fractured the stock of his rifle by stamping on it. As an extra cause for annoyance, the journey to Ghadames should have covered 800 kilometres; in fact, they travelled 1,600. When asked why he had chosen such a devious route, Babani replied that there were bandits in the area; this was the only way of avoiding them. He may have been right, but Laing did not trust him.

At the next habitation, Insalah, there was more trouble. Although it was an important stopping place on the routes taken by Arab caravans, the inhabitants hated foreigners. When Laing came among them he caused a sensation. How, they asked, had this Christian infidel dared to enter the town? For such impertinence he must

* A collection of people travelling across the desert – not to be confused with the tiny houses on wheels used by gypsies and holiday-makers.

die. Sheik Babani did nothing about it and Laing's life would have ended there and then – had it not been for a young nobleman named Sidi Othman.

Just as the population of Insalah was drawing its swords, Sidi Othman came to the rescue. Laing, he explained, was a perfectly harmless individual and it would be cowardly to kill him. They ought to be ashamed of themselves. The anger subsided. Laing was allowed to go on his way.

He had been hoping to go to Timbuktu, to proceed down the Niger to its mouth, and to return to Tripoli by ship in time for Christmas. But the year was running out and he had still a long way to go. In three months they had covered less than a quarter of the route; and, although Laing professed to be in excellent health and spirits, he must have been disappointed at the slowness of the expedition. All the letters he sent back to Tripoli stressed how much he was missing Emma. When Warrington managed to send him a portrait of her painted by the Spanish Consul, he became wild with anxiety. If the picture was accurate there could be no doubt that 'my Emma is ill, is melancholy, is unhappy – her sunken eye, her pale cheek, and colourless lip haunt my imagination'. Perhaps it was not a very good likeness. Nothing suggests that she was unwell.

Another letter gave voice to his suspicion that Babani and his followers were trying to trick him. This, quite likely, was true.

They were now passing along the edge of the Agahaggar mountains – the spine of the Sahara. The landscape was almost unearthly. In its wildness and its apparent lack of life it seemed to belong to some other planet. But somewhere behind the rocks, in the sharp

creases of a hill, or crouched in some unseen valley, there
were members of the Tuareg tribe.

To the unprepared European traveller the Tuaregs
were as lethal as the scorpions which infested the desert.
Of all the tribes they were the most fanatical about
keeping foreigners away from a world that (or so they
believed) had been created by Allah exclusively for
Moslems. Since it was unlikely that anyone else would
have wanted it they were, perhaps, unreasonable. But this
mistrust was ingrained in them. They killed as a matter
of principle – as instinctively as they might scratch an
insect bite.

Christmas had come and gone without being noticed.
On a night in February 1826 the caravan was encamped
at a point 240 kilometres south of an oasis. At three
o'clock in the morning a rifle shot broke the deep silence
and then there was the sound of men running. The
bullet hit Laing as he lay asleep, piercing his side and
grazing his spine. He managed to get to his feet – just as
a party of Tuaregs threw themselves into his tent. They
were all armed with swords. A quick thrust in the thigh
sent him to the ground. He was unarmed and completely
helpless. He struggled to get up; another sword slashed
at him, cutting his cheek and ear. Simultaneously a heavy
blow broke his right arm just above the wrist. Bleeding
heavily, he fell down again. They closed in on him and
dealt him seven more cuts before – believing him to be
dead – they departed. While this was taking place, his
servant was hacked to death. The rest of the caravan,
which included Sheik Babani and his followers, was
unmolested.

How had the Tuaregs known exactly which was
Laing's tent? Somebody, surely, had betrayed him. If

the attackers had been bandits the whole encampment
would have been ransacked and everyone slaughtered.
But this, obviously, was not an act of armed robbery.
Laing and his attendant were singled out because they
had dared to trespass.

By some miracle Laing survived. Sheik Babani was
obviously the man who had betrayed him to the Tuaregs,
but now he showed compassion. He carried him for
320 kilometres to the camp of Sheik Sidi Mokta. Sidi
Mokta was friendly and sympathetic. Laing must rest
until he felt fit once more. His arm was broken; his jaw
was fractured; his face was permanently disfigured; and
there were something like twenty-four cuts on his body.
It would be some time before he could resume the
journey.

Without the assistance of skilled medical attention the
process of recovery took three months. But the troubles
were far from done. A few days after they had left Sidi
Mokta, Babani complained that he was feeling unwell.
Laing, too, experienced the beginning of a fever –
though he thought the terrible ache in his head was due
to his injuries from the Tuaregs. Other men took to their
beds, and it soon became clear that they were suffering
from typhoid. Babani and three others died; Laing,
against all probability, recovered. Now, when his energies
were at their lowest ebb, the last of his personal
attendants refused to go any farther. Still running a high
temperature, he arranged for the man to return to
Tripoli. 'I told him he might go,' he wrote. 'I blame
nobody for taking care of [himself], so in God's name let
him go. I have given him a camel, provisions, etc. So that
he departs like a sultan.'

He was now utterly alone except for Babani's men.

They looked a villainous bunch and they probably were. But they had become impressed by Laing – by his bravery, his extraordinary powers of recuperation, and by his determination. For the rest of the trip they remained loyal to him. On 18 April, standing on top of a sand-dune, he saw his objective. There, only a few miles away, were the houses and minarets of Timbuktu.

After nearly a year in the desert the market place for slaves and gold seemed as luxurious as a Mediterranean resort. Babani's son found him rooms on the upper floor of a two-storeyed mud house. After a month, he had made friends with some of the town's intellectuals and he was enjoying himself. Despite the fact that he had to use his left hand to write, he managed to draw a street map of Timbuktu. He also began to plan his journey to the mouth of the Niger. It was clearly not going to be easy. His friends told him it was too dangerous. The governor took a stronger line: he forbade him to undertake the trip. He must return to Tripoli by the route he had come – and the sooner he departed the better it would be.

Unaccountably, the mood of Timbuktu, which had been pleasant, even hospitable, had suddenly turned against him. He was no longer a guest but a hated Christian whose very presence poisoned the air. The time to get out was now, before the threats and the mutterings turned into physical violence. He sat down at a table and wrote his last letter. It ended with the words: 'I regret to say the road is a vile one, and my perils are not yet at an end.' He departed with a negro slave whom he had freed and an Arab boy who wished to visit a port on the Niger. The next day or so are obscured by mystery.

Despite the governor of Timbuktu's objections, his plan was still to trace the Niger to the sea. He intended to travel overland to Sansanding, where he hoped to embark on a boat. But Sansanding lies to the south-west of Timbuktu, whereas Laing travelled northwards to Arawan. Did he change his itinerary at the last minute? Had news of his unpopularity been carried downstream, making it impossible for him to find a suitable craft? Did he, therefore, intend to follow the governor's instructions and return to Tripoli across the desert?

It is possible. At Arawan the Sahara caravan routes came together. One led to Fez in Morocco, the other into Tunisia. Unfortunately the reason for his decision will never be known, for Major Alexander Gordon Laing completely disappeared.

Two years later, long after Laing had been given up for dead, another European reached Timbuktu. He was a Frenchman named Réné Caillie and he survived the experience by taking suitable precautions. He not only disguised himself as an Arab, he also learned the language. When he returned from the city sandwiched between sand and swamps he travelled with a caravan of 1,400 camels transporting slaves, gold, ivory, guns and ostrich feathers. Nobody seems to have discovered the intruder in their midst.

On Caillie's return he reported that Laing had indeed been killed. According to the story he had been told, the unfortunate Scotsman had been strangled by negro slaves. He was taken to the spot where the deed had been carried out. 'I averted my eyes from this scene of horror,' he wrote, 'and secretly dropped a tear – the only tribute of regret I could render to the ill-fated traveller to whose memory no monument will ever be reared on the spot where he perished.'

But Réné Caillie's account was untrue, and many more years had to pass before an accurate version of Laing's last days came to light. It was discovered by another French explorer, Bonnel de Mezières. In the early twentieth century M. de Mezières travelled to Timbuktu, expressly to investigate Laing's death. While he was there he spoke to an ancient Moslem who was the nephew of the Scotsman's murderer. No, he was not slain by native slaves. This man was sure of it; for, as a boy, he had often heard his uncle tell the story.

It seemed that, when he arrived at Arawan, Laing was seized by a small team of assassins who had been sent from Timbuktu. Their leader, a fanatic named Labeida, began by insulting him. Then he demanded that he renounce Christianity and accept the Moslem faith. Laing refused. He knew that such an action might spare his life, but it would not get him back to Tripoli. He would spend the rest of his days as a slave in the desert. Even death would be better than that.

Labeida was impatient. When Laing turned his proposition down he signalled to one of the other Arabs. The man drove his spear through the Scotsman's chest. Then they beheaded him and set fire to most of his possessions. The Arab boy was also killed; the negro slave was wounded and taken back into captivity.

If he wanted proof de Mezières could examine Laing's grave. There it was, by the side of the trail, underneath a palm tree. It contained the remains of the unfortunate man's body and one or two personal possessions that were easy to identify. They had, it appeared, been buried by a passing tribesman. Labeida and his fellow villains had left their victim to rot in the sun.

Poor Laing: if only he had disguised himself as Caillie had done. But that wasn't his way. He was much too proud.

4 The Prince of Evil

There is no point in looking up Moara Pahou in an atlas; it is not marked. Nowadays it may not even exist. In 1879 it was a village with a hundred houses surrounded by rice fields, gardens in which pineapples grew, banana trees and sugar canes. If one could endure the almost unbearably hot and humid climate it was rather a pleasant place. The pineapples, according to one traveller 'were especially delicious, and nowhere have I tasted sweeter and more juicy'.

Moara Pahou did nothing to influence world affairs. It produced no famous men and women, it caused no international incidents, and it never became industrialized. It was a place of no importance except for one thing. It was here that a Dutch explorer named Carl Bock came face to face with one of the most evil men in the world.

Bock was travelling in the Dutch colony of Sumatra (now part of the Republic of Indonesia) when he received a message from the governor. He was to proceed at once to Borneo and explore the south-eastern portion of the island. The director of the educational department in Batavia gave him his final instructions. It was obviously going to be a long and hard journey, so he would need servants. Bock was prepared to pay good wages but nobody was willing to accompany him. He approached Dutchmen, Malays, Chinese and half-breeds; they all refused his offer. Perhaps he was not being sufficiently generous. He increased the amount, but still nobody came forward.

What, then, was wrong? Somebody, surely, was prepared to endure the rough life of an explorer – especially when so much money was waiting to be earned. Eventually, when even the superintendent of police had failed to find any recruits, he discovered the answer. People were afraid. Borneo was the land of the Dyaks and, as everyone knew, these people were head-hunters. Common sense was more powerful than the spirit of adventure; the urge to live was greater than the promise of good wages.

Presently Carl Bock set off alone for Borneo. He had plenty of supplies, including a quantity of tinned foods. He managed to recruit five servants when the ship called at Surabaja, but they were not very satisfactory. Three lads, who came from Java, suffered from acute home-sickness; one of two Chinamen threatened to desert, the other demanded constant pay rises. It was really a form of blackmail but Bock was in no position to argue.

Whatever stories may have spread to the rest of the East Indies, Borneo was not peopled entirely by savages. Many of the coastal areas had been colonized by Malays who were ruled by a Sultan. The Sultan turned out to be an amiable character who was anxious to help and extremely hospitable. Though, like all true Moslems, he was a teetotaller, he offered Bock champagne and proudly showed him his fabulous collection of diamonds.

The Malays worked hard and farmed well. They even ran a coal-mine – though the miners were mostly convicts. Still, it was no doubt preferable to the settlement's other form of punishment – flogging. Since the Sultan could not rely on anyone else to carry it out with suitable brutality, he had appointed his two sons as executioners.

Eventually Bock, travelling mostly by river, arrived at Moara Pahou. It was the last of the Malay villages: beyond it any pretence of civilization ceased and the dark, mysterious land of the head-hunters began. Carl Bock was a conscientious explorer. Some people might have considered they had gone far enough. The prospect of decapitation was sufficiently terrifying, but an even worse fate was possible. Most of the Dyaks contented themselves with keeping a stock of human heads handy for use on ceremonial occasions. There was, however, one tribe – the Trings – who went a good deal farther. As the people of Moara Pahou made haste to tell Bock, they were cannibals. His instructions from the Sumatra government surely did not insist that he should end up in a stew pot?

But Carl Bock refused to be daunted. If the worst came to the worst, he was adequately armed. Fortunately it did not; for, if a shooting match had occurred, the Dyaks would probably have come off best with their blowing-tubes. Not only were they extremely accurate but their darts, which were tipped with poison, were lethal no matter where they struck.

This venom was taken from the sap of the Upas tree. Death was not instant. At first the victim became listless and suffered from a mild irritation. The best that could be said was that it produced no great pain. Presently his breathing slowed down. This was followed by convulsions and then, some while later, by a paralysis that spread over the body. When it reached his heart he died.

Bock had hoped to meet some Trings at Moara Pahou;

but when he arrived there were none of them in the
village. As he saw the situation there was only one thing
to do – visit them on their own ground. The Sultan, who
had turned up, tried to dissuade him. It would, he said,
amount to certain death. They would not regard Bock
as a lone explorer who came as a friend. On the contrary,
they would assume that he was the advance guard of a
large force assembled not only by the Malays – but
also by tribes who had unwillingly contributed to the
Tring menu. But Bock was adamant. 'I explained,' he
wrote afterwards, 'that I must see them, having heard
so much about their atrocities and cannibalism. The
Government would expect me to report on these savages;
and I should be to blame if I did not see them, both men
and women.'

When two reasonable men find themselves in a state of
disagreement a compromise is sometimes possible. On
this occasion the Sultan saw the point of Bock's
argument. Rather than risk losing such a valuable guest,
however, he decided to send some of his own men into
Tring territory. Travelling in a large canoe with a
reliable officer in charge they were to invite a deputation
from the cannibal kingdom to visit the village.

Six days passed. No Trings arrived and, more
worrying, the canoe did not return. Plagued by
thoughts of his men being killed and cooked, the Sultan
sent off another canoe. This time a senior officer was put
in charge and the crew were heavily armed. Three days
later they returned in convoy with the earlier party. The
two craft had forty tribesmen on board – including four
women.

While they were at Moara Pahou the Trings were kept
in a compound, and it was noticeable that other Dyaks

went to a good deal of trouble to avoid them. They spoke a language of their own, but fortunately the commander of the second canoe – a veteran captain who had once served the Sultan as a tax collector – understood it. Among the women was a priestess. When Bock questioned her about her life-style she made no excuses. 'She told me,' he wrote, 'holding out her hand – that the palms are considered best eating. Then she pointed to the knee, and again to the forehead, using the Malay word *bai*, *bai* (good, good) each time to indicate that the brains, and the flesh on the knees of a human being, are also considered delicacies by the members of her tribe.'

From the Trings Bock learned a good deal about head-hunting in general. Far from regarding it as a villainous sport, the last word in barbarity, they insisted that their tribal customs depended on it. Nor could they see what all the fuss was about. During a war that had lasted from 1859 until 1864 the Dutch forces had killed Dyaks and Malays by the hundred. The motive, as Bock's informant saw it, was entirely one of greed. 'Why, then,' he said, 'should they object to our killing a few people now and then when our custom requires it? We do not care for the instructions of the white men, and do not see why they should come into our country at all.'

It was a point of view with which it was difficult to argue.

All cannibals were head-hunters as well; but by no means all head-hunters were cannibals. This grim ritual came into a Dyak's life from the moment he was born until the day he died. Heads had to be produced when he was named. Early on, a youth was given a sword, but he was not allowed to wear it until he had washed the blade with blood. He would go on his first head-hunting foray at the age of fifteen. He was not, however, considered qualified until he had attended four of the expeditions. Nor was he allowed to smoke or marry until he had accounted for at least one head.

Indeed, so far as courtship was concerned, the more heads he could produce the better. This was explained by the simple fact that every Dyak girl wished to marry a hero. It was a poor kind of warrior who could not produce one – if he could display six or seven he was much more of a man. Given a good score, he could depend on being accepted by the young lady of his choice.

When a chief died a reasonable parade of heads was considered essential. They were not there as ornaments but for a much more sensible purpose. When, as go he must, the chief went to heaven, the heads' decapitated owners would serve as his slaves.

The best way to obtain heads was to do battle with a neighbouring tribe. The rules of the game insisted that they must be enemies, though no previous history of hostility was required. If you charged into the village waving swords and lances, you and they became, so to speak, instant foes. It was as simple as that. The cannibals explained that they did not eat human flesh as a regular diet – but only as a ritual carried out after these raids. They were probably speaking the truth.

Before going out in search of heads the tribesmen performed a ceremonial dance. Two of them, clad in war dress, walked round and round, using long strides and stamping the ground. At first they kept at a distance from each other – gradually drawing closer until, at last, they became locked in combat. Using the blunt sides of their sword blades, they carried out a mock fight, uttering savage yells with the spectators joining in. On some occasions they wore masks shaped like alligators' heads. There was nearly always a musical accompaniment played on a kind of two-stringed banjo and a flute.

The final act, before setting out on the quest, was a confession of sins by all the men and women in the village. For lesser crimes the penitents were fined a fowl or a pig. More serious offences were punished by the culprit being deprived of salt, or fish, or even his or her clothes.

On the journey to the hunting ground, runners kept the warriors in touch with the village. If anyone died the expedition was postponed and they trooped back for the funeral. Such delays sometimes lasted for several weeks.

In the best military tradition the attack usually took place shortly after dawn. When the killing stopped, the heads of the dead were removed and dried over a fire. These became the property of the chiefs. In the case of cannibals, lesser beings had to content themselves with the victims' flesh.

When at last they returned to the village, the outing was celebrated by a feast that lasted for ten days.

During the forays a number of prisoners were usually taken. They were brought back as slaves – and also to provide an emergency supply of heads for occasions such as the death of a chief. The executions were carried out with suitable ritual. A stake – about the height of a human being and sometimes topped with the carefully carved likeness of a human head with its tongue out – was set up in the centre of the village. The victim was lashed to it. Accompanied by a dismal wail uttered by the priests and priestesses (both sexes could achieve this

exalted rank, and the women were the more influential
of the two), the warriors advanced on the unfortunate
individual. Using their lances, they inflicted one wound
after another for about an hour. By that time the slave
was nearly always dead – usually from loss of blood.
Afterwards his head was chopped off.

Of all the tribes, the Trings were the most brutal.
Their nominal ruler was a character named Raden Mas,
but he was not typical. He had given up cannibalism in
order to adopt the Moslem religion. The official reason
was that the Sultan had insisted on it. According to
Bock, however, a more likely cause was that he liked the
idea of having more than one wife. He dressed himself
in a neat cotton jacket with gold buttons and a pair of
shorts. 'He was,' Bock wrote, 'compared with his
second-in-command, Sibau Mobang, quite a
gentleman.'

Sibau Mobang was undoubtedly the prince of
darkness; the most evil man in the world. Even his
appearance was enough to chill the spine. He was one of
the Trings who came down river in the two canoes. Bock
received him in a house that had been put at the
Dutchman's disposal. The arch-cannibal was
accompanied by two women and three men; he seemed
to be about fifty years old. Wrote Bock, 'I was hardly
prepared to see such an utter incarnation of all that is
most repulsive and horrible in human form.'

His face had a yellowish-brown, rather sickly
complexion. His eyes displayed 'a wild animal
expression, and around them are dark lines, like shadows
of crime'. He had, apparently, lost all his teeth and his
right arm was paralysed. For this reason he wore his
sword on that side and wielded it with his left hand.

The meeting seems to have been uncomfortable. The Dutch explorer was shocked at Sibau Mobang's reputation; the Tring leader seemed to be rather shy. But this may have been because he had just returned from a hunting trip. All told, or so he said, he had accounted for seventy victims. Yes – they included women and children.

Sibau Mobang smiled only once during the encounter. That was when Bock, who was a good artist, showed him a sketch he had made of him. Could he keep it ? The Dutchman politely said 'no', but custom called for some exchange of gifts. He presented the Tring with some dollars, strings of beads and twenty-four yards of calico. They were, he said, to be divided up among the visitors. Sibau Mobang, in return, gave the Dutchman a couple of human skulls – each minus the lower jaw. Then, rather grudgingly, he handed over a shield made from wood and decorated with his victims' hair. No doubt some museum eventually became the proud possessor; they were not the kind of ornaments one likes to have at home.

Carl Bock eventually completed his journey of exploration and returned to Holland. For the Dyak head-hunters, however, the big adventure was yet to come. It began on the day they died. Considering the brutality with which they lived, it may seem strange that they had such strong ideas about an after-life. There were several different stories about the long road that led to heaven – all of them impressive exercises of the imagination.

For example, when a dead Dyak steps into the world beyond, he wanders from here to there until he arrives

at a river. Before he can cross it he must build himself a canoe and a paddle. On the far side he comes to a mountain, which he must climb. Somewhere on the slopes he meets a member of his tribe.

There is still a long way to go. Presently, he descends into the valley of tears where he meets several men, women and children. He must give clothes to each of them. Coming out of the valley he encounters a giant caterpillar, which he must feed from a special plant.

Another mountain stands in his path. This, too, must be climbed. On the way up, there are a great many flies and he is met by a large bear. The animal must be offered a pig. And so he travels on, meeting more human beings, all of whom have to receive presents, until he comes across a woman crushing rice. She asks him to help her, but he must refuse and quicken his pace. At last, after passing a fire in the middle of the road, jumping over some tree trunks, and meeting a woman whose ears are so large that they provide shelter from the rain, he reaches yet another mountain. This is bigger than the others; as he starts to climb it, he feels, for the first time, that he no longer belongs to the living world. At last a narrow road takes him into a forest where his parents – accompanied by a strange woman – are waiting for him. They tell him to bathe in a nearby river; but there is yet another mountain ahead. This is the final obstacle. When he has climbed it he is given some fruit to eat. He has, at last, reached the heaven of his tribe.

A chief, of course, has an easier journey, for he is accompanied by the spirits of his slaves – without any heads, presumably.

5 From East to West

You have, no doubt, heard of Billy the Kid ? Jesse James ? Wyatt Earp ? But do the names Meriwether Lewis and William Clark mean anything to you ? Perhaps not, and this is one of the strange things about the legends of the American West. There are many stories told, and films made, about the villains – who, in these epics, become translated into heroes. But these two men, who marched into the unknown and actually discovered the West, are mere shadows.

Meriwether Lewis was born in Virginia on 18 August 1774. When he was a youngster he spent much of his time exploring the woods around his home. He loved remote places and he learned how to fend for himself. In a city he would have been less than happy, but in the wilderness Meriwether Lewis was at home.

Soon after his twentieth birthday he joined the army. For the next few years he served on the frontier – the border-line between the last traces of civilization and a huge expanse of country that had never been explored. Somewhere beyond it lay the Pacific Ocean. Of the land in between, people knew nothing. According to some theories, a waterway, beginning at the mouth of the Mississippi, cut the continent into two. They called it the North-West Passage.* If it existed there would be no

* Not to be confused with another North-West Passage, that was believed to link the Atlantic to the Pacific around the north of Canada.

need for ships to sail from one ocean to the other via South America and round Cape Horn.

In 1801 Meriwether Lewis was called to Washington where he was appointed private secretary to President Thomas Jefferson. To be taken from the wild country he loved so much, and to be put behind a desk, may seem to be an unkind stroke of fate. But President Jefferson had his reasons. He had known Lewis as a boy in Virginia, and he had followed his military career carefully. During this period the adventurous Captain Lewis was, in fact, being prepared for a much bigger task.

In 1792 an explorer named Robert Grey (who was, incidentally, the first United States captain to sail round the world in an American-built ship) visited the mouth of the Columbia river on the Pacific coast. He had established a claim to the region, and to the fur and fishing rights. Jefferson felt it would be strengthened if a United States expedition made a journey to Grey's landing place across the continent from the east. It was, he believed, possible that the Columbia joined the Mississippi, and that the entire trip could be made by water. But, whatever the situation might be, he proposed to put Meriwether in charge.

No doubt about it, the project was ambitious. If it was to succeed, one thing was essential: access to the Mississippi. At the end of the nineteenth century this huge river, which enters North America at New Orleans and meanders through Louisiana, did not belong to the United States. The tracts of land on either side were owned by the French and governed by the Spaniards.

In 1803, the French – who had troubles enough elsewhere in the world – suddenly decided to sell

Louisiana to the United States. The asking price was
$23,213,567 and 73 cents. Jefferson snapped it up. He
and his fellow countrymen were now the proud
possessors of an extra 23,310 square kilometres –
111 square kilometres more than all the land they had
previously owned. It was a bargain. What's more, the
way to the west was now open.

By the time the Louisiana Purchase had been
completed, Meriwether Lewis had attended a college in
Philadelphia and studied botany, zoology and celestial
navigation. At some point, he suggested to the President
that there should be two officers in charge of the
expedition. He named William Clark, who also came
from an old Virginian family, as a suitable companion.
Jefferson agreed. Lewis was 29 at the time; Clark, 33.

Originally it had been intended to send twenty men on
the trip. When they began to make preparations,
however, Jefferson decided that this was not enough.
There should be at least forty. The type of people
needed were 'good hunters, stout, healthy, un-married
young men, accustomed to the woods'. There would
have to be carpenters among them, and men who could
repair guns and others who could handle boats.

With the exception of nine watermen, all the personnel
enrolled by Lewis and Clark came from the army.

There was much to be done. The men had to be
specially trained. A great many stores (including presents
for the Indians, a swivel gun and an air gun) had to be
assembled, and the boats had to be built. Lewis ordered
a large vessel, fifty-five feet long and propelled by
twenty-two oars, from a yard at Pittsburgh, plus a couple
of large canoes constructed from the hollowed-out trunks
of trees. Among the stores there was ammunition, tools,

1,681 kgs of pork, 1,542 kgs of flour, and quantities of oatmeal, salt and biscuits. Lewis's Newfoundland dog, Scannon, was to go with them. Clark was accompanied by his negro slave, York.

Jefferson gave Lewis detailed instructions about the information he was to bring back. He was to learn all he could about the characters and traditions of the Indian tribes. He was to keep a sharp eye open for commercial opportunities and to find out about the climate, the geography, the plants and the animals. He must also consider whether the country through which they passed would be suitable for settlers.

They spent the winter of 1803 making preparations. On 14 May 1804, at four o'clock in the afternoon, the expedition departed up the Mississippi from St Louis. A gentle breeze filled the boat's square sail; with the two canoes following obediently in its wake, the tiny fleet presently rounded a bend in the river and vanished from sight. More than two years were to pass before Lewis and Clark were seen again.

Some miles above the town the river divides, and the Missouri streams away to the west. They decided to follow it. At first, the going was comparatively easy. There was plenty of wild game to be shot on the banks; this, and fish fresh from the river, made sure they had plenty to eat. The pork could be kept in reserve for the coming winter. As for the Indians, they seemed to regard them with curiosity rather than hostility. There was one uncomfortable moment when a party of Sioux tried to turn them back. As their leader explained, they suspected them of carrying arms to the tribe's enemies upstream. With the aid of an interpreter, Lewis managed to put their minds at rest. They were allowed to proceed

without menace – and with no need to man the swivel gun.

By 2 November they had reached a group of Sioux villages about eighty kilometres from the Canadian frontier in what is now North Dakota. The weather was turning cold, and Lewis and Clark decided the time had come to go into winter quarters. The next stage of their journey would have to wait until the spring.

The carpenters got out their tools, while the others went into the forest and chopped down trees. Before very long they had built five reasonably comfortable log cabins in a place they named Fort Mandan. The neighbouring Sioux Indians seemed friendly; they accepted gifts and were grateful for the medical attention that Clark and Lewis provided. The days of angry Indians fighting equally angry cowboys were still a long way off.

Clark and Lewis had been instructed in medicine, though their remedies were not very elaborate. They either bled their patients, dosed them with medicine that caused them to perspire, or else they purged them. If the ailment did not yield to one or other of these treatments, there was little they could do. At Fort Mandan Sergeant Charles Floy suffered what was probably an acute appendicitis. Despite the combined efforts of Lewis and Clark, his condition grew worse – until presently he died. They were more successful with an Indian girl named Sacajawea. She was married to a French-Canadian named Toussaint Charbonneau, and she was having difficulty in childbirth. Lewis got hold of the idea that the powdered rattle of a rattlesnake, taken in water, might assist matters. To catch one of these deadly reptiles was hard enough, and the remedy sounds more likely to kill than to cure. But in Sacajawea's case it worked. She produced a fine, healthy boy – who was named Jean-Baptiste.

It was the perfect introduction. They soon learned that Sacajawea belonged to another tribe that inhabited the land ahead of them. At the age of 15 she had been kidnapped by the Sioux. Her husband, Toussaint Charbonneau, was one of many hunters and trappers who came down from Canada. Indeed, when they were at Fort Mandan, an Englishman arrived to offer his services. He was politely turned away.

There were many things to be done. They built six more canoes out of strips of willow; chopped quantities of wood to feed their fires; and went out on hunting trips. Lewis and Clark wrote up their reports on the journey so far, illustrated them with maps and drawings, and prepared the specimens of natural history that Jefferson was so anxious to obtain. The time passed quickly, and then it was April.

Lewis liked the place, and described it as 'one of the fairest portions of the globe'. He had little idea of what lay ahead. Indians who had come into the camp spoke of mountains, and suggested that they would be unable to make the entire trip by water. At some point they would probably need horses. But they, too, were vague about conditions beyond Sioux territory.

As soon as the ice covering the Missouri had melted, the large boat, manned by sixteen men, set off back to St Louis with the reports, maps and specimens. Before the rest of the expedition resumed its journey Charbonneau told Lewis that the best people to provide horses would be the Shoshoni Indians – the very tribe from which Sacajawea had been kidnapped. On condition that they might bring their baby son with them, he and his wife agreed to come with them. They might not be the best of guides but they would be ideal negotiators.

The Missouri was now nearing its source in the mountains and the journey became harder. On one occasion they had to fit wheels (made by slicing tree trunks into sections) to the canoes and trail them eighteen miles over rough country. At various points on the route they hid consignments of stores for use on the return trip.

With every mile, or so it seemed, the navigation became more difficult. Dams built by industrious beavers blocked the narrow waterway; there were boulders in mid-stream and treacherous banks of gravel on which the craft grounded. The Missouri, certainly, was not to be the North-West Passage on which the President set so much store.

Before long the canoes had to be abandoned and they travelled by foot. As they struggled up the lower slopes of a mountain range, they could have done with an Indian guide. But the Redskins kept their distance. Clark and Lewis saw no signs of them at all – though, by all accounts, they were being shadowed by braves who made the maximum use of cover. At last Lewis picked three men to accompany him, and announced that they would go on ahead of the column as a scouting force. Presently they saw a member of the Shoshoni tribe standing alone on top of a hill. Lewis called to him but the man fled. However, it was enough to show that somewhere in this wilderness of rocks and peaks there were people. He ordered the rest of the expedition to come up and join him.

On 12 August they reached the top of the Lembi Pass,

2,247 metres above sea-level in what is now called
Montana. They were drenched by the rain, cold from the
eternal frosts, and very hungry. Some of the men were
ill – and just as the rattlesnakes had been a threat at lower
altitudes there was now the menace of hungry grizzly
bears. But the military discipline which Lewis and Clark
had enforced throughout the trip held the expedition
together. In such harsh surroundings there was no
sense in deserting. On the other hand, who knew what
lay ahead ? A bad situation might easily become worse.
It must have been tempting to turn back, but nobody
considered doing so. No matter what dangers the
unknown had in store, they were all determined to face
them.

Near the Lembi Pass they came across a group of
Shoshonis. The Indians were suspicious, and when
Lewis asked them to accompany him, they refused.
Every expedition needs a miracle now and again ; this
was when Lewis and Clark had theirs. By an
extraordinary coincidence, the group's chief was
Sacajawea's brother. After a joyous reunion the
Indians supplied them with horses, and even gave them a
young brave, whom they named Toby, to act as a
guide.

Toby brought them to a trail that was used by his
fellow tribesmen when they went down to the plains to
hunt for buffalo. It was an improvement, but only just.
In places there were large patches of ice which caused
the horses to slip ; before long early snowstorms added
to the difficulties. What was more, they were already
discovering an uncomfortable truth about this uncharted
land. It was known that a range of mountains walled
off the rest of North America from the Pacific. What

nobody had realized was that, in fact, there were two – one running parallel to the other.

Sick, famished, and very tired, they clambered over the Rockies and then trudged across the Clearwater range. Eventually they came to a valley. The sides were a strange shade of brown and nothing grew on them. But if there seemed to be no end to the wilderness, at least the trail led downhill. Before very long they met more Indians. This, surely, was a good sign.

By now they were too weak to defend themselves. If the Indians had decided to steal their horses there was little they could have done about it. In fact, these braves belonged to a tribe known as the Nez Percé – so-called by French trappers because they wore shells in their noses – and they were extremely friendly. They provided them with food and escorted them to a point where the trees began again and where a ribbon of water departed on its journey to the west.

The barrier had been pierced and the way to the Pacific was clear. They would now be able to travel by boat again, and Lewis and Clark put their men – now in much better shape – to work felling trees and carving out the trunks to make more canoes. When they were ready, the Nez Percé Indians offered to look after their horses until they returned. The men were so obviously trustworthy that Lewis gratefully accepted.

Most of their problems were over. The Snake River, as that encouraging lane of water was called, brought them to the Clearwater, which brought them to the Columbia. On 15 November 1805 they reached its mouth in what is now the state of Oregon. Again the carpenters became busy as the others supplied them with logs. Presently a collection of huts surrounded by a stockade was completed. It was situated a few miles from the ocean. They called it Fort Clatsop.

Another winter had to pass before they could begin their return journey. But, knowing the way and prepared for its hazards, they fared better this time. On the eastern side of the Rockies, they divided – with Lewis taking a more northerly route and Clark following the Yellowstone River. On 23 September 1806, united again, they sailed triumphantly down the last stretch of the Missouri, and then along the Mississippi to St Louis. The only casualty during the entire expedition had been the unfortunate Sergeant Floy. On the way back Lewis was wounded in the backside – by accident. He was bending over at the time, and one of his hunters mistook his buckskin breeches for an elk.

Sacajawea had shown herself to be just as tough and fearless as the men. Once, when a large canoe overturned, she salvaged all the contents. She was also an expert in digging out suitable roots to augment the supplies of food.

As they approached St Louis, Lewis wrote, 'We suffered the party to fire off their pieces as a salute to the town, we were met by all the village and received a harty welcom [sic] from its inhabitant &c.' He and Clark were each rewarded with 648 hectares of public land; the men who had served under them received 130 hectares and double pay. For them, at least, the expedition had a happy ending.

However, as time went on, the Red Indians fared less well. Perhaps, given enough imagination, the shape of the future could have been seen on the lower stretches of the Missouri. The country on the right-hand bank was inhabited by a tribe named the Poncas. There had once been several thousand of them. By the time the two explorers and their men went by, the number had been reduced to two or three hundred. These were the only survivors of a smallpox epidemic. The disease had been introduced, like so many other ailments, by the white settlers.

The Indians found the white man's attitude hard to understand. In 1855 for instance a Nez Percé chief was offered money for his land. He refused. According to his belief nobody owned the earth. How could a man sell something that was not his?

But by this time most of the tribes were already being herded into reservations by unscrupulous settlers who were hungry for territory, or gold, or both. Those Indians who did try to defend their rights were made immortal when the cinema industry began. Even somebody who does not know what a Red Indian looks like would have no difficulty in identifying them. They are always shown as villains. But that is the unjust thing about the West. Its real villains have been turned into heroes; its real heroes, such as Lewis and Clark, have been forgotten.

6 Gold Fever

The town looked like a piece of cheap jewellery that had been dropped beside a huge stone wall. Despite the fact that it was not yet dark, it glittered with electric lights. There was, too, a rough and ready design about it. The streets were laid out in neat blocks; here and there the lines of small wooden houses were broken by the intrusion of an hotel or a theatre. To be sure, the place was small, but it seemed to have everything. Perhaps the best way of describing Juneau, Alaska, in that early summer of 1897, is to call it a miniature city.

No matter at what hour of the day or night you arrived there, Juneau always seemed to be busy. Somebody was selling something, and someone else was buying it. The merchandise may have been furs, or sealskin boots, bottles of whisky or groceries – did the shops ever close? The town was only six years old but in places it was already shabby. No wonder – half the world, or so it seemed, had come there, stopped for a few nights, and then moved on. Everyone had the same idea: to make a fortune. Juneau was the gateway to a land of gold.

Wherever you went in the town you heard tales of wealth. The hoteliers and the shopkeepers had never *seen* such torrents of money. At Selby's Smelting Works men who were shabby and who looked tired emptied sacks of gold dust on to the counters. The clerks used copper scoops to transfer these small shining hills on to the scales. When they translated the weight into its cash value the amount was enormous. The men smiled happily. They had done what they set out to do.

Every time the little steamer *Excelsior* eased herself away from the quay for another journey up river, her decks were crowded. On the return trips there were fewer passengers. If you studied their faces and conversations carefully you could notice a difference. The men departing from Juneau had an excitement, an innocence, about them. Somehow they seemed to be younger than those on the way back. Their faces reflected hope, whilst the others suggested experience. The veterans of the gold fields knew that the truth was not in the noisy, rackety town – but in those towering mountains that lay behind it.

In September 1896 a prospector named George Cormack had discovered a rich lode of gold at Bonanza Creek on the Klondike River. You had, it appeared, only to go there and help yourself. But was it really so easy to become rich ? Some people may have doubted it, but not many. Men left their homes, their jobs, selling everything they had to pay the expensive steamer fares to Alaska. A physician in St Louis set about building a balloon. When it was completed, he said, it would carry fifty people. Tickets for a trip into the heart of the Yukon would cost $240 each.

A lady from Chicago set off for the land of promise with a hand-operated printing press. She was, she said, not so much interested in the gold. But she intended to give the Klondike its first newspaper. At San Francisco, a rather shrewder character chartered a ship for $35,000 – and made a profit of $65,000, on the first voyage.

Behind it all, there was a kind of madness. So many of these hopeful people had not the slightest idea of what to expect. Some took their bicycles with them. A farmer brought two horses and a plough (they were, after all, gold *fields*), and an English clergyman wanted to know which was the nearest railway station to the Klondike. Few seemed to realize that, between Juneau and the gold, lay some of the cruellest country in the world.

It would have been better if they had shared the experience of one hopeful gold-digger. On his way to the Klondike he had come across a man lying in the snow. His head was resting on a large sack, and he appeared to be asleep. When he looked more closely, however, it became obvious that the man was dead. The sack was crammed with gold dust, and yet he had died of starvation. In this part of the world a loaf of bread was worth more than a mass of yellow metal. It was a grim sight, but it was also a warning.

But the stories of the failures, the tragedies, the men who got it wrong, were seldom told. People wanted to believe it was easy to become a millionaire, and they much preferred the one about a stoker from one of the ships. This man had been earning a paltry $8 per month. One day, he packed up his belongings and set off for the diggings. When he returned, he had made $170,000.

Of course, when you were thousands of miles away in your sitting room at home, it may have seemed easy. You picked up an atlas and looked for the name 'Yukon'. There it was, a fine, broad river that joined the Klondike near a place called Dawson City. It shouldn't be hard to get there: after all, quite large steamers plied on rivers such as the Mississippi.

If the Yukon had been like the Mississippi, or the

Thames, or like any other reasonable river, there would have been no problem. But it wasn't. There were rapids and whirlpools, and for nine months of the year it was frozen over. In 1897 the only way to the Klondike was overland – and that meant over mountains.

This was the reality, but who wanted to know about it? Hadn't a party of sixty-eight miners gone to the Yukon from Portland, Oregon? And had they not returned with over a ton of gold? They had brought it back in sacks and blankets, baskets and boxes, and they had sold it for $1¼ million. This was the kind of thing people liked to hear about.

And so they set off in swarms for Juneau, and some of them didn't even take sufficient utensils in which to bring back their rewards. One man carried his gold dust to Selby's in a rusty can that had once contained tinned fruit; others used jars in which jelly had been preserved. You could even see miners tipping the stuff out of paper bags on to the mahogany counters.

Of course, not all the gold came as dust. Nuggets the size of hazel nuts were said to be commonplace. Cram your pockets with them, and you became wealthy. It was common knowledge that in Juneau you could buy the essential equipment – a pan, 46 cms in circumference and 10 cms deep – for $3. For such a simple item, which was really no more than a sieve, the price was outrageous, but what else did you require? Well – there were other things, such as food and warm clothing, and tools and tents and, possibly, a team of dogs. According to one expert, if you set out for the Klondike and hoped to come back alive, you should spend at least $300 on equipment – and then there were the steamer fares on top of that. They were extortionate: even if you had the cash it was sometimes difficult (especially in June, which was the best month) to buy a ticket. At places such as Victoria, British Columbia, San Francisco, and Seattle, people sometimes waited on the quayside all night – simply to be sure of a passage.

But, despite all the difficulties, egged on by the magic word 'gold', the world flocked to the Klondike – and some of the world never came back. In 1897 the road (which is not really the word, for there was no road) from Juneau to Dawson City was such that even an experienced explorer would think twice about going there. Nevertheless, a contemporary photograph shows a mountain pass covered in snow. Some of the stretches to the top are almost vertical; and yet, down the centre of the picture, there is something that looks like a grey stream. Study it more carefully, and you see that it is a long, long queue of people. On one occasion the authorities reported that there were 18,000 would-be gold-miners literally clogging the route. When at last they reached the edge of the land of opportunity, some of them went mad. Throwing away their packs and provisions, they ran helter-skelter to the rivers where the precious metal lurked.

Alas – the tragedy of it. Anyone could find gold, but there was no replacement for food and clothing; and, without it, there was no way back to Juneau.

The dirty little steam launch *Excelsior* from Juneau had been built to carry twenty-five people. Now, with the demand for tickets so great, the skipper took a new look at his vessel and decided it could accommodate fifty-five. Crammed together for a voyage that covered one hundred miles, the passengers must have had their first doubts. With so many people obviously out to grasp gold, would there be enough to go round? They needn't have worried. This would be the least of their problems.

At a place named Dyea the *Excelsior* landed her load of humanity, took on board returning miners with their sacks of wealth, and chuff-chuffed back to Juneau. The new arrivals looked about them at this hastily erected staging post. The view was not encouraging. There was a store made out of logs and a scattering of tents. It all seemed very far from the comforts of Juneau. What was more, the landscape in front held no encouragement. About thirty-nine kilometres away, a giant white wall interrupted the pattern of snow-covered mountain peaks. This was the awesome Chilcoot Pass. As the residents of Dyea cheerfully explained, the gold fields lay on the far side.

If you needed help Dyea was your last opportunity to obtain it. Indians of the hardy Thlinkit tribe were prepared to offer their services as porters. They made up the loads in packs of 45 kgs each. The rate for carrying one pack over the Chilcoot was between nine and twelve dollars. But some people preferred to move their belongings on a sledge pulled by dogs. The price of one animal was $75, but it was best to use a team of four. That cost $300. After the stop at Dyea on top of the stay at Juneau, most people *needed* to strike gold; for, by then, they were almost broke. That, indeed, was one of the things about the Gold Rush: the number of tradesmen and dealers who made their fortunes without going anywhere near the fields.

A rough trail led from Dyea to Sheep Camp at the base of the Chilcoot. It was possible to ride along it, but Sheep Camp was the end of the road. After that you had to walk. Walk? Perhaps – though 'clamber' would be a better word.

To begin with, the route led through the trees. There was a pleasant scent of evergreens and the slope, whilst becoming steadily steeper, was really not too bad. But the trees eventually petered out, and there were still more than a thousand feet to go. The journey took at least three hours. It was intensely cold. Even in June there were sudden snowstorms, and patches of dense mist, which were just as bad. They came without warning, and settled over the pass in a damp, chilling, stinging cloud, as if each was made up of millions of particles of ice (which it probably was). For three hours, or more, it blotted out everything. The only thing to do was wait.

Some people suffered from frost-bite; some died of exposure through not wearing suitable clothes; some simply threw away the hope that had brought them to this terrible place, and died of nothing.

This part, near the top of the Chilcoot, was the worst. You had to scramble up a wall of ice on your hands and knees, then over a vertical wilderness of loose boulders. If you dislodged one, and it was easy to do so, it might hit somebody lower down. But by this time you could count yourself lucky. You had avoided the deep crevasses just beyond the tree-line, which were concealed by thin layers of snow. You had even negotiated a particularly nasty bit, where stones and ice seemed determined to make you slip – and where, if you did so, you fell three hundred metres before you died. But you were now at the top. If you had hired Indian porters you praised your own good sense. If you had not, you were completely exhausted – too tired, indeed, even to feel sorry about the false economy.

It was tempting to regard the Chilcoot Pass as the big barrier between man and gold; to imagine that, if there were no mist, it would be possible to stand on top of it and see the Klondike River. In fact, crossing it only accounted for a small part of the journey. Those who had travelled light, and entrusted their baggage to the porters, often discovered that their troubles began on the far side. Quite often, they had to wait several hours until their possessions arrived. Sometimes the Indians staged a lightning strike for higher rates of pay. Since it was difficult to move on without their assistance, they always won. In any case, by this time, their clients were beyond caring. What, after all, was money? In these surroundings there was too much of it to be discovered, and too little for it to buy.

After crossing a range of smaller hills, and then wading through a river that was often so swollen by heavy rains that it was apt to sweep people off their feet, you arrived at a lake. In winter, of course, it would have been easier: you could have crossed the river by walking over the ice. But nobody who was not either exceptionally brave, or else exceptionally foolish, would have attempted the Chilcoot at that time of year.

Some travellers took the precaution of buying what were advertised as 'Yukon Boats' before setting out. For those who had not done this there was now a difficult task ahead. Somehow, they had to build one. In the early days, provided a man had the tools and the skill, it wasn't too difficult. The lakeside was covered with trees: it was just a matter of chopping one down and working on it. By mid-1897, however, most of the trees had gone, and it was a question of walking several miles in search of timber. If an aspiring miner had forgotten to bring any tools he had only two alternatives. One was to persuade somebody else to give him a ride (almost impossible – what with baggage, equipment, and the boat's owner on board, there was no room for passengers). The other was to turn back, facing again the dreadful wall of rock and snow that is the Chilcoot.

In mid-summer, the rest of the way to the Klondike was by water. The shores of the lakes and rivers were thickly wooded and the woods were inhabited by wolves and bears. Now and again a member of one or the other species would peer out between the trees, watching with mild amusement the antics of these not very able seamen.

Some people were better at building boats than others. Some found the task impossible and tried to construct the next best thing – a raft. It is doubtful whether many of them ever reached their destination. A vessel needed to be reasonably seaworthy to make the trip. There were sudden storms, hidden rocks and, worst of all, the White Horse Rapids. This turbulent stretch of water, which thundered between rock walls thirty metres high, became known as the 'Miners' Grave'. At the end of it there was a sad little collection of stone cairns and wooden crosses, marking the resting places of those who'd been drowned in the angry river.

At last, given strength, warm clothing, enough food, a strong boat and a lot of luck, the gold-hungry travellers reached the Klondike. They may have stopped at Dawson City; some of them went on to a place misnamed 'Forty Mile City'. It was doubtless forty miles (sixty-four kilometres) from somewhere, but even the least critical of visitors could not have called it a city. It was a collection of about eighty log huts, an hotel and a saloon, a so-called Opera House (one doubts whether the management had ever heard of Gilbert and Sullivan, let alone Mozart and the rest), stumps of sawn-off trees and a sickening amount of rubbish. Bread was nearly always scarce. In winter, with the temperature outside at about −50°F, it was almost impossible to keep warm. In summer swarms of mosquitoes infested the place, and the wise man went about with a mask on his face and gloves on his hands. The only good things to be said about it were that there was plenty of whisky and very little crime. A detachment of Royal Canadian Mounted Police stationed in a small barracks suffered from nothing worse than boredom.

Having survived so many ordeals, it should now have been possible to look for gold immediately. But – no. It is a simple rule of life that, wherever there is an opportunity, it will not be long before an official turns up. After all, the prospectors were after money; the shopkeepers, the bar-keepers, the show girls and the hangers-on were after the prospectors' money; it was surely only reasonable that the poor State should also have some. That, at any rate, was how the mind of government worked – and still does. Small men with forms and pens move in; and before you can say 'Eldorado' there is a System.

In this instance the miner had first to call at an office and apply for a 'Free Miner's Certificate'. Of course, it wasn't free at all, it cost $5. But this was cheaper than paying out $25 which was the penalty for not having one. You were now permitted to look for a vacant claim. If it was on the shore of a lake or a river, it would be 150 metres long. Elsewhere it was thirty metres square. It had to be marked out by four posts – each, for some reason, at least 10 cms square. On one of them you had to write your name, the date, and so on.

Then you returned to the office. The claim had to be registered; naturally this cost more money. A kind of entrance fee of $25 had to be paid, plus another $100 for every year you worked there. The land and the gold it contained was now all yours – or almost. If you left it for seventy-two hours – say you became ill, for example – you lost your rights and somebody else could take it over.

It was one way of making a fortune – but at what a price!

At the height of the Klondike gold rush the population of Dawson City was 25,000. By 1903 the excitement was all over and it had dwindled to 3,000. Nowadays only 881 live there. As time went by, ways of reaching the gold fields were improved. Twenty stern-wheelers ran a service for three months of the year up the Yukon River, and they managed to build a narrow-gauge railway over the mountains via the White Pass, which was less steep than Chilcoot. Nevertheless, searching for gold in this sub-arctic territory was always difficult, always uncomfortable, and often dangerous.

7 Escape to Square One

In January 1882 the Royal Geographical Society decided to send another expedition into the centre of Africa. The society's council selected a young Scottish explorer named Joseph Thomson as leader. The object, he was told, was to see whether it was possible to travel from the east coast to Lake Victoria. There were many obstacles on the way, and the greatest was a tribe named the Masai. They were known to be unfriendly to foreigners: the question was – would they let Thomson pass through their land? If they did, it would become possible to open up the heart of the continent to commerce and missionaries. But this was not Joseph Thomson's only task. On the way he was instructed to take a detailed look at Mount Kenya, and, said the council, 'make all practicable observations regarding the meteorology, geology, natural history, and ethnology (*the characteristics of the people*) of the regions traversed'. It was a tough assignment – the hardest and most dangerous that this adventurous young man had ever undertaken.

Africa killed Joseph Thomson, and this expedition had a hand in it. In fact, the Scottish explorer died in London on the second day of August 1895. But Africa was responsible – just as much as if a native warrior had been sent to drive a spear through his heart. Joseph Thomson perished from too many attacks of fever, too many hardships and too much danger. It was the penalty for travelling into the unknown.

When Thomson reached Mombasa he quickly discovered how difficult the expedition was going to be. Everybody, or so it seemed, was outward-bound towards the heart of the continent. A German named Dr Fischer had recently set off along a route similar to the one he proposed to take. A collection of missionaries and merchants was preparing to go. The result was that all the reliable guides, interpreters, and porters had already been recruited. When Thomson announced that he intended to march through the heartland of the Masai, nobody was interested.

In desperation he increased his offer of wages by one dollar per day per man. One or two natives looked at him with mild curiosity; nobody became excited. When he said that no matter how dark a man's past life might be he would ask no questions, the result was better. Eventually, 110 came forward. They were not the ideal companions for such a trip. Some of them were former convicts – others would have been, if the police had discovered them. Most were anxious to get away from the city and its forces of law and order. The ideal number for such a venture was 300 but this was out of the question. Similarly, if he had been doing things according to the book, he would have had six experts to perform the joint functions of guide and interpreter. He could enlist only two – and a couple of mean and crafty rogues at that.

Happily, he was more fortunate in his choice of a white companion. When he left England he had determined to travel alone apart from the porters. But in Mombasa he struck up an acquaintance with a sailor from Malta named James Martin. For the past six years Martin had been working at a mission in the town. Now he was out of work. Would Thomson give him a chance? He understood the natives, could speak about ten languages, and had no fear of the dangers and discomforts. What was even more important, he was enthusiastic about the idea. It was more than could be said of the others.

Thomson signed him on, and he never had reason to regret it. Afterwards he wrote that Martin was 'always cheerful . . . and he had no opinions of his own'. It was, it seems, 'an admirable quality for a subordinate in an African expedition'.

On a day in March 1883 Thomson, Martin, the 110 porters and three donkeys set out from Mombasa. To begin with, the going was not particularly difficult. The trouble would come when they reached the approaches to Mount Kilimanjaro. This enormous piece of natural architecture, 5,890 metres high, which stands near the Kenya frontier with Tanzania, was perhaps a symbol. It was as if the word DANGER were written on its eternally snow-capped peaks. Beyond Kilimanjaro lay the world of the Masai. Anyone who ventured into it did so at considerable peril.

Things might have been better if the Royal Geographical Society had provided the expedition with more money. Despite the fact that Thomson was accompanied by only one-third of the number thought essential for such trips, he had been short of cash. The Masai, it was presumed, were like all the other inhabitants of Africa's interior. Proud warriors though they might be, they would be glad to receive gifts. Indeed, there was more to it than that: they would *expect* to receive them in return for a safe conduct through their land.

Joseph Thomson had beads and bales of cotton and
ironmongery, but he had nothing like enough. Indeed,
his supplies of hardware for the natives were
depressingly small: there were not enough porters to
carry an adequate amount. Nevertheless, the promise of
passing through the Masai lands unmolested was
essential. He and his men were, admittedly, well armed.
But if it came to a fight with the tribesmen, they would
be outnumbered, outmanoeuvred, and generally
outclassed.

As they approached the territory they began to
receive news, and all of it was bad. Dr Fischer and his
300-strong caravan had, it seemed, already passed this
way. Fighting had broken out and a Masai woman
had been killed. This was appalling. The Masai waged
a continuous, almost traditional war with another tribe
named the Lajombe. If the warriors of one side came
across the men of the other all hell was likely to break
loose. Even so, this was a strangely civilized conflict.
Man-to-man, it might be a fight to the death; and yet
the women were allowed to go about their business in
peace. A Masai would no more think of hurting a
Lajombe woman, than a Lajombe would consider
harming a female member of the Masai clan. It was out
of the question.

But now the unforgivable crime had been committed,
and the person responsible had been a white man. The
Masai leaders had never seen one of these strange and
pallid creatures before. They were not eager to allow
any stranger to pass through their territory; there was
certainly no special welcome waiting for unknown
intruders, who might just as well have come from another
planet. Fischer had been compelled to hand out presents

on an above-average scale but he had got away with the
crime. He had such an army of attendants, and they were
so heavily armed, that even the Masai warriors, fearless
though they were, had been prudent. The fate of
Thomson and his motley crew might be different.

If you fell into conversation with Joseph Thomson
two phrases were apt to crop up. One was an Italian
saying with which he illustrated his cautious approach
to problems. The words were: 'Who goes slowly, goes
safely. Who goes safely, goes far.' It was no doubt very
sensible, but then he would refer to 'my lucky star'. He
had, he professed, great faith in it. If there was any
conflict between caution and optimism the latter would
almost certainly win. The fact that Dr Fischer's shooting
match had ruined the chances of striking up an amiable
relationship with the Masai did not deter him at all.
Ill though the omens might be, he would press on.

However, when he pitched camp that night he took
the precaution of surrounding it with a wall of wood.
One couldn't be too careful.

Three days went by before there were any signs of the
Masai being aware of their presence. Tension within
the camp mounted. Although Thomson and Martin
went bravely about their duties they, too, must have
been nervous. If the Masai warriors attacked them their
rifles would be more effective than the native spears.
They might even be able to escape. But the empty
scrubland ahead, and the bland flanks of Kilimanjaro
to the east, gave no clues about when this would happen.
As on all such occasions, the waiting was the worst part.

On the fourth morning the suspense was broken as a
number of Masai women approached the camp. They
had, it seemed, been on some sort of shopping expedition

for food. When they noticed the tents their curiosity was aroused. They were dressed in skins and were wearing masses of beads and bracelets. More important, however, were the bunches of grass they held in their hands. As one of Thomson's interpreters hastened to explain, these were emblems of peace.

The women seemed eager to talk. A deputation of the tribe's leaders would be arriving next day. At present they were discussing what should be done with the intruders. The meeting was far from unanimous. Some were in favour of slaughtering them in revenge for the woman's death: others took a more reasonable line. They should be allowed to proceed on their way – in return, it went without saying, for a lavish supply of gifts. There had been much argument and one or two fights. By the following sunrise they would have reached some sort of agreement. Until then Thomson and his men would have to wait.

The day passed; night fell; and at last the sun rose on the far side of Kilimanjaro. Presently a strange sound came from the nearby forest. It was almost as if the trees were singing in a great arboreal choir. Since stretches of African woodland are not in the habit of bursting into song there was only one thing to make of it: the Masai were on their way, chanting as they marched.

Thomson's men prepared to receive them. The outcome might be peace or war. The men were prepared for either: in one hand each clutched his gun – in the other, a bunch of friendly grass. When at last the warriors could be seen, they turned out to be superb physical specimens who carried themselves with immense dignity. Thomson was impressed. 'What splendid fellows!' he later noted in his journal.

Each was armed with a spear and protected by a shield. For the moment, however, they did not seem anxious to use them. They stuck their spears into the ground and solemnly sat down with their chins resting on their knees. Thomson sat on a camp stool, and his men, still holding their firearms, lined up behind him.

There was a lot of chattering between one Masai and another until presently a spokesman rose to his feet. He was holding some sort of cudgel which he used for gesturing with eloquent effect as he spoke. This, at last, would be the moment of truth. If these men were a sample of Masai warriors, heaven help Thomson and his followers if the verdict went against them.

According to the ideas of the day, the strange dark men of the desert and the forest were 'savages'. It was a word that was ill suited to these delegates of the tribe. They regarded the intruders into their country with a singular lack of interest. They were aloof, even haughty. The white man's magic (whatever *that* was) held no magic for them. They were polite, one had to admit, and yet Thomson could not help feeling that they were treating him in much the manner they might treat a slave.

The spokesman crisply outlined the situation. One of their women had been shot by another stranger, and it had seemed sensible that the married men of the tribe should decide their fate. There had, he admitted, been some very angry argument. But eventually they had decided against another outburst of violence. The white men and their retinue might pass through the land in peace. There were more speeches from both sides; but for the moment things were looking good.

Everybody has his breaking point; the moment when his dignity crumbles. For the warriors, it came when

the gifts were produced. Suddenly, these exquisite
specimens of humanity, these men who seemed to be so
sure of their power and their magnificence, became
transformed into a greedy pack of ruffians. They fought
and they scrambled and they grasped, each intent on
helping himself to the largest share of the loot. One of
them was seriously injured in the affray but nobody paid
any attention.

At last it was over. The warriors recovered their
dignity once more, and spent the night peacefully in
Thomson's camp. The first round was over. The
expedition could continue.

Next day they began to explore the lower slopes of
Mount Kilimanjaro. Unfortunately, when they made
camp some while later, it seemed as if the decision of the
chiefs had not been circulated to the rest of the tribe.
Or had they changed their minds ? They had passed
Masai villages unmolested; without, indeed, anybody
showing any interest in them. But now there was
something vaguely ominous in the air. It was hard to
explain it; some subtle difference in attitude that made
Thomson feel uneasy.

People had flocked into the camp and the distribution
of gifts was made. But on this occasion the visitors did
not seem to calm down afterwards. There was none of
the politeness, the dignified condescension of a superior
being speaking to a lesser mortal, that had marked the
attitude of the chiefs. Thomson was feeling weak after
an attack of fever and he had intended to remain in his
tent. But now there was a lot of activity at the entrance
– as if the Masai were trying to break into it. The patience
of his men must be wearing thin; and he knew very well
how disastrous it would be if one of them fired a shot

in anger. Feeling depressed and irritable he went outside and sat down on a box.

Hitherto, the Masais' interest in the white man had seemed to be very small. Suddenly the attitude changed. They compelled him to remove his boots; they laughed at his clothes; they forced him to wiggle his toes; they mocked his fair skin and his hair. It was intensely humiliating – rather like being a slightly comical exhibit in a side show. But, unless there was to be fighting, he had to remain patient.

The crisis came when one warrior, drunk with beer made from honey, tried to remove his trousers. Thomson could stand no more and he gave the man a push. The Masai's face twisted with fury. Retreating a pace or two, he drew a knife. Then he sprang forward. Thomson neatly side-stepped, and two of his men grabbed the attacker. For the sake of diplomacy they tried to calm him down, but he was beyond reason. Eventually they threw him out of the camp.

But there were worse things in store. Reports now came in that suggested the chiefs had, indeed, changed their minds. An army was massing ahead of the expedition, intent on barring the way. Whilst they would be safe enough in camp, the odds in a running battle were entirely in the Masais' favour. In any case, Thomson told himself, he had been sent to this part of Africa to explore – not to fight. Somehow he and his men would have to creep away from this damned spot, to get back to the coast and buy more, many more, gifts and recruit more men. They had come in too small a number; their supply of presents was too small; and, after the distressing experience of Dr Fischer, they had come too late.

In exploration, as in other games, you sometimes had to go back to square one.

Thomson made his plan carefully. Apart from telling his men that the fires must be kept burning, and that there must be no changes in the routine, he took nobody, not even James Martin, into his confidence. Since he had already begun to mistrust his two interpreters, he was probably wise.

At nightfall the last of the Masais left the camp and returned to their kraals. Two hours later, after giving hasty instructions, Thomson ordered his men to march. He would lead; Martin would bring up the rear. There must be absolute silence – especially since they would pass close to several villages.

There were thick clouds overhead. Somewhere in the area of Kilimanjaro a thunderstorm was raging. There were crashes of thunder and, now and then, a particularly vivid flash of lightning. Thomson had only a compass which he tried to read by means of a lantern concealed beneath his jacket. It began to rain.

Even in daylight the going would have been horribly rough. Now, in this utter darkness, it was almost impossible. They stumbled over stones, were cut by thorns, and tumbled into holes. He may have despised his bearers as an unruly and often mutinous bunch of villains. On this occasion, doubtless because their lives depended on it, their discipline was superb.

They marched, and marched, and marched. The thunderstorm from Mount Kilimanjaro overtook them, drenching them and adding to the store of anxieties. Each fork of lightning that stabbed the earth lit up the scene; for a split second it was as bright as noon. Then merciful darkness returned.

During these instances of illumination, surely they could be seen by the Masai warriors who guarded the villages. They listened for the war chants, the thud of men running in pursuit, but there were no such sounds. The enemy, for that was what they had become, preferred to stay indoors on a night such as this. One could hardly blame them.

When the sun came up they were almost exhausted. Nearby there was a native village. Was this a Masai outpost, or were they now in safer territory? Thomson sent one of the interpreters to investigate. When he returned, he could see that their troubles were over. The inhabitants, it seemed, were friendly. They even offered to sell the expedition some food. The road back to square one was now clear.

Joseph Thomson's lucky star had not deserted him. He and the rest of the expedition returned to the coast, re-equipped themselves, and set off again. On 10 December of that year, after another and more successful journey through Masai territory, they accomplished their goal of reaching Lake Victoria.

8 The Long Drive

The argument had gone on for many days. The two men seldom became impatient. Sometimes they gave the subject a rest; and, for a while, made polite and aimless conversation. But they always returned to the matter – each determined to win.

It would be hard to imagine two characters with less in common. One of them was an Italian prince named Scipione Borghese. The other, Na-Tung, was President of China's State Council. Borghese was a nobleman with perfect manners, a sensitive face and a sharp intelligence. Na-Tung was a villain. Seven years earlier someone had described him as 'one of the most dangerous men in Asia'. It was a fair assessment, for Na-Tung was one of the minds behind the Boxer Rebellion of 1900.

The object of the rising had been to expel all foreigners from China. The German Minister in Peking was murdered and so were several missionaries. For nearly two months representatives of the diplomatic corps were besieged in a corner of the city – until, on 14 August 1900 an international army came to their rescue.

Afterwards Na-Tung went into hiding. Despite several demands for his execution he managed to remain alive. Indeed, he did more: when tempers cooled, and the rebellion was consigned to history, he wriggled back into favour. Now, next to the Dowager Empress, he was probably the most powerful person in China.

But the subject of the argument was not power or politics; it was concerned with a motor race. In March 1907 the Paris newspaper *Le Matin* had challenged motorists to drive from Peking to Paris. The distance was at least 16,000 kilometres and in many places there were no roads. What was more, cars were a great deal less reliable than they are today. None of them, surely, could withstand such punishment?

Many of *Le Matin*'s readers believed that they could. When, however, the newspaper insisted that everyone taking part should lay down a deposit of 2,000 francs, the enthusiasm waned. Eventually five contenders arrived in Peking. Of the cars one was a little three-wheeler; there were two 10-hp de Dions, a 15-hp Spyker driven by a Dutchman, and a 40-hp Itala with the 35-year-old Prince Scipione Borghese at the wheel.

The prince had already made his name as an explorer. He had crossed Persia on the back of a camel; with some assistance from the Trans-Siberian Railway he had travelled from Europe into Asia, and thence to the Pacific. There was no doubt about his courage; but he was not, simply, a man who delighted in adventure. His mind was cold, scientific and practical. His published account of his exploits was not the kind of thing you read for excitement. It was more like a textbook.

At his meetings with Na-Tung he needed all his coolness. If he became impatient he might just as well return to Italy and *Le Matin* would have to call off the race. The point was that Na-Tung and his colleagues on the State Council refused to allow the cars through their country. They had several good reasons – all of which centred around their dislike of the 'Chi-cho' (as they called such vehicles; it meant 'fuel chariot', and was not

to be confused with 'fire-chariot', which meant
'railway').

The Chinese government had invested a lot of money
in constructing a fire-chariot system and it did not want
any competition from upstart motor vehicles. What was
more, it was afraid these 'diabolical machines' would
unsettle the minds of the peasantry. Finally, Na-Tung
could not see the point of the race. Nobody in his right
mind would wish to travel from Peking to Paris by such
a horribly uncomfortable method. Since the prince and
his friends were obviously not mad, there must be some
hidden reason. It did not take the wily politician long to
decide what it was. These men were foreign spies! On
no account must they be allowed to run their race.

But the prince was stubborn and he argued well.
After a while Na-Tung began to yield ground. The
motorists might be issued with conditional passports.
Conditional? Yes – provided they travelled by an
impossible route through Manchuria. Borghese shook
his head, and drank another cup in the endless ritual of
tea-drinking.

At last he managed to wear down Na-Tung's
resistance. The Chinaman suddenly shrugged his
shoulders and rose to his feet. Very well, if they wished
to make such an insane journey he withdrew his
objections. It was madness, but foreigners *were* mad. In
any case, they would not get very far. The whole thing
would come to a wretched end amid the mountains in
north-west China. The fuel-chariots would never get
beyond *that* barrier.

Strangely enough, the prince was not worried. If they
failed to penetrate the mountain range it would, at least,
prove something. He had already ceased to think of the

event as a race. It was more of a test – something to discover what could (or, of course, could not) be done with a motor car under extreme conditions. Whatever happened, they would end up knowing more about this method of locomotion.

Once Na-Tung had given his consent the Prince became very busy. In six days he covered about 480 kilometres on horseback: studying routes, organizing dumps of fuel, even conscripting camels to carry stores. So far as he could, he did his best to convince the people they had nothing to fear from the strange mechanical monsters that would soon be coming through their villages.

At last, on 10 June 1907 everything was ready. At eight o'clock on that rain-drenched morning, the small cavalcade of motors lurched over the pot-holes on the road out of Peking. At the end of this first day the three-wheeler gave up the struggle. It had travelled 64 kilometres over a road that was wet, slippery, and carved up into huge ruts. In company with the other vehicles it had been manhandled over a large marble bridge built 600 years earlier on the instructions of Marco Polo. To judge by its condition, it had not received any attention since. The ramps on either side had been snatched away by flood water, and the bridge itself was beginning to crumble.

The three-wheeler had retired; the others were now depending more on man power than on horse power. According to Borghese, during the first 240 kilometres they only covered fifty under their own power. For the rest, they were pushed by coolies and pulled by horses. It was, perhaps, a little unfair to suggest that such experiences revealed shortcomings in the vehicles' designs. They were among the mountains that Na-Tung had believed to be impassable. The men who had dreamed up the de Dion, the Spyker and the Itala, had certainly not envisaged such cruel ordeals for their brain-children. Nor, when they established their primitive trails through the mountains had the Chinese said, 'We'd better make them good – one day, perhaps, a motor car will come here.'

On the far side of this terrible country lay the Gobi Desert. There was a lot to be said against it. The sun blazed down for day after day, never winking, never hiding behind a cloud. In places the route was marked by the bones of long-dead animals and men arranged in neat piles. Were they intended to indicate a direction or a warning? For most of the time the drivers were too hot and bothered to care. Without exception, they were all suffering severely from sunburn.

But the Gobi had two blessings to offer. Whatever its shortcomings, it was flat. The surface was tolerably firm and the cars could travel under their own power. In places they cruised along at 48 kph. It was not exactly a world record, but the Gobi Desert had not been built by nature for speed events.

The other advantage occurred at a village named Pong-kiong on the edge of the desert. When they arrived there they found that a small telegraph station had been installed in a mud hut. Somebody had put it there six years earlier – and then, presumably, forgotten about it. At any rate, so the local inhabitants said, it had never been employed. Borghese and his companions were grateful for it. They used it to send messages, reassuring their wives and well-wishers that they and their cars were still alive and well. Since nobody in

T–DJ–D

Pong-kiong knew how to work the apparatus they tapped out the telegrams themselves. Despite its neglect, the equipment worked.

Presently the desert petered out, and they drew near to the frontier with Russia. The going now became difficult again; by the time they crossed over into Siberia the Itala and the Spyker had both been hauled out of bogs. Nevertheless, the four cars were still in good working order. The hardest part of the trip was surely over: having come this far it was reasonable to hope that they would reach Paris.

Reasonable? Perhaps. But the journey through Siberia was obviously not going to be easy – or comfortable. On the first night, they put up at a small inn. By the following morning all four drivers were itching from the tops of their heads to the soles of their feet. The rooms, it was horribly clear, had been infested with bugs. Afterwards they slept out of doors. It was bitterly cold but at least there were no insects.

The citizens in this part of Siberia had never seen a car before. They regarded it with interest and soon conceived the idea that it had commercial opportunities. When Borghese tried to charter a ferry to take them across a lake the boatman said that the price would be 300 roubles. Since this was several hundred per cent more than the normal rate, it was out of the question. Scipione Borghese might have been a prince of the blood royal, but he was not a fool. The others could do what they liked: *he* proposed to motor round the lake.

As the ferry-keeper was very well aware, there was only one clear route along the shore, and this had already been occupied by a railway line. Chortling to himself, he decided that it would not be long before the prince returned. He would then be made to pay for his pride: the fare would be increased to 400 roubles.

It simply goes to show how little he knew about Borghese. Far from capitulating, the prince approached a railway official and asked for permission to drive over the tracks. The man considered the idea crazy; but at least it might provide himself and his colleagues with a little innocent amusement. Life in this part of Siberia was not very exciting; the idea of this stranger and his extraordinary contraption wobbling over the sleepers had some very humorous possibilities.

Much to the surprise of one and all (well, not quite all – the prince had been full of confidence), the Itala played its role of a one-truck railway train very well. It was only when they were approaching the end of the line that any trouble loomed in sight. As obstacles go it was fairly substantial for it took the form of a train approaching from the opposite direction. However, there was a siding nearby. A signalman deftly switched the points over, the car was shunted out of the way, and the express roared past.

Near the siding there was a road, and the road pointed in the right direction. Borghese decided that he had run on rails for long enough. Helped by the railwaymen, the car was hoisted off the track and set down again on its natural element. The engine sparked and settled down to a happy growl, Borghese waved a gesture of thanks and drove off down the highway. Before very long he came to a bridge. It looked sound enough, but when he was halfway across he discovered that the timbers were rotten. It had never experienced a weight such as the Itala's before. With a groan and a snap and a wrench and a crash, it collapsed. One moment the car was trundling over the planks: the next, it was marooned in a torrent.

If the railway workers had been disappointed by the lack of drama during the Itala's progress over the permanent way, this more than made up for it. They rushed to the spot, extracted the prince and his servant from their watery predicament, and then – with great physical strength – hauled the car ashore. By one of those miracles that sometimes favour the brave, neither the car nor its crew were damaged. A little wet perhaps; the Itala's bodywork scratched and dented a bit, but nothing more serious.

The hazards were still not yet over. Some miles ahead they were stopped by a soldier. There had, it seemed, been a spot of bother. A minor revolution had broken out in the neighbouring town of Irkutsk. The rebels had captured the barracks, seized the arms and released the convicts from Irkutsk's prison. They were now believed to be lurking in the woods. Would the prince and his companions like to have a military escort ? The prince said they would not. It would slow them down too much. After all, this was supposed to be a race.

Borghese's optimism was justified. Only one shot was fired that night – by a trigger-happy Cossack who aimed his revolver at the Itala's headlamps. Thankfully he missed.

Civilization was at hand. The prince's first glimpse of it came as he approached the border of European Russia. It assumed the solid, rather comforting shape of a steamroller that was working on a new stretch of highway.

For part of the way ahead, traffic travelled by boat along the River Volga. To do likewise would obviously be cheating. There was only one snag: with everything going by water nobody had bothered to build a road. The Itala made the best of some very heavy going; but at one point it was too much. With what seemed to be a sigh the car entered a marsh – and sank in up to the tops of its wheels.

But at last the soggy progress was concluded by the coming of good roads, and a trouble-free run all the way to Paris. At four-thirty p.m. on 10 August the Itala and Prince Borghese triumphantly entered the city to the applause of a large crowd. They had won the Peking–Paris race by a handsome margin – to be precise, by a matter of three weeks. Nevertheless, despite his success, the Prince doubted whether a car journey between the two cities was a practical proposition. Of the 16,000 kilometres covered, 12,000 had been over rough tracks. Such a trip might be all right for adventurous people such as he and his fellow competitors. For anyone who cared about comfort it was impossible.

Na-Tung no doubt smiled when he heard about the prince's opinion. He had known that it was almost impossible. During those long sessions of cups of tea and argument he had said so – many times.

9 Whatever became of the Colonel?

In a manner of speaking, the story began in 1743. A Portuguese adventurer named João de Silva Guimarões was leading a party of men through the unexplored interior of Brazil. Presently the jungle cleared; ahead of them they saw a line of mountains. There was something uncanny about the peaks. When the sunlight hit them it appeared to bounce back. To Guimarões it looked as if they were made of glass. Beyond this crystal range, perhaps, lay the fortune in gold and silver he was seeking. But no matter how hard he studied it, he could see no way across. At last he gave up. He told his companions to pitch their tents. Next day they would turn away from this unfriendly wall and retrace their steps towards the east.

If it hadn't been for a white stag, that would have been the end of the matter. At some time round about dawn the animal broke cover. Two of the men, who were gathering wood, spotted it. They picked up their guns and hurried off in pursuit. If they managed to kill it there would be enough meat for the present and for several days to come.

The stag escaped; but before they lost sight of it they came across a track leading to a pass in the mountains. The two men hurried back to camp and awakened Guimarões. They had found the crack in the wall – the way ahead was now clear.

For these men, who were inexperienced climbers, the

going was rough. Here and there, however, they found traces of what seemed to be paving stones. Was it some ridiculous trick of the imagination, or had this once been some kind of thoroughfare?

At last they reached the top. In front of them, hemmed in by towering white peaks, there was a wide valley with a stream parting its carpet of pale green grass. But there was more – much more. In the centre of this depression there was a city. Guimarões and his men were now frightened. This was no Indian village: the houses were tall and stately. There were three massive arches at the entrance – and, beyond, an avenue as grand as anything in Europe. For the better part of an hour they lay there watching and listening. But the only noise was the sound of the wind; the only movement was the rippling grass. There was absolutely no sign of people.

Holding their weapons tightly, they cautiously approached the arches. There were still no signs of human life. Surprised but now feeling safer, they set off up the avenue. Halfway along it they came across a fine square, marked by a stone obelisk at each corner. In the centre there was a huge black column capped by the statue of a man. He had one hand on his hip; the other was pointing northwards.

It was now becoming uncomfortably clear to Guimarões and his followers that, whilst there might not be any people in the place, it was not entirely empty of life. The buildings were inhabited by bats. In an explosion of dark wings they flew into the street, creating a fearful noise and beating against the men's faces. The furry fliers appeared to have taken the place over. Having expelled the human population they were determined that no man should ever again occupy it.

The explorers retreated and moved off along the river. At one point they found a gold coin; at others, nails made from silver. Nine days later they saw a canoe in the distance. It was occupied by two white men. They had loose black hair and, incredibly, they were dressed like Europeans. One of Guimarões's attendants fired a shot to attract their attention. It must have scared them for they paddled harder and were soon out of sight.

Guimarões wrote an account of his discoveries. As soon as he and his men came across another track leading towards the east, he sent the document by runner to the Portuguese Viceroy at Bahia. Nothing more was ever heard of the explorer, nor of this strange deserted city, and certainly nothing of this race of white men that travelled in canoes and lived so close to heaven.

Many years later a colonel in the British Army named Percy Harrison Fawcett came across Guimarões's manuscript. It was another clue to a puzzle on which he had been working for some time. Perhaps it was the most important; the others had been legends – this one was a collection of facts recorded by a man who was obviously not very good at writing – and not very imaginative. Improbable though it was, he felt bound to believe it.

Colonel Fawcett had been commissioned into the Royal Artillery in 1886. He was a tall man – 1·87 metres – and unusually strong. He had been a good athlete with a modest reputation as a boxer. As an artist he was talented enough to have had his drawings hung in the Royal Academy. But this was still not the sum of his accomplishments. He had once built a couple of racing yachts without any help.

No doubt about it, Percy Harrison Fawcett was a very unusual man. He had the most lively imagination; by religion he was a spiritualist, and he enjoyed an uncanny immunity from illness. In South America he worked in swamps and jungles where fever was rife, but he only once fell sick. He was, he said afterwards, ashamed of himself for this lapse. During World War I he served on the Western Front with such courage that he was awarded the DSO. In peacetime, he had spent much of his career on loan to the Bolivian Government. His task had been to survey its frontiers with Brazil and Peru.

This was the kind of life that appealed to Fawcett. With his considerable stamina and his inquisitive imagination he was a born explorer. He preferred the rough life of the jungle to the comforts of towns. What was more, it gave him plenty of opportunities to study the legends passed down from one generation of Indians to the next. These stories all seemed to indicate the same thing: thousands of years ago, long before the Incas, there had been a race of white men living somewhere in Brazil. The evidence of Guimarões surely confirmed the fact and encouraged a theory that was growing in Fawcett's mind. Here, he believed, was the edge of the lost continent known as Atlantis.

Was there ever such a place? A vast slab of land in what is now the Atlantic Ocean, peopled by men and women whose armies overran the Mediterranean countries? According to Fawcett's theory, they became immensely powerful and very rich. Presently, driven by an insatiable appetite for pleasure, they began to worship evil gods. Not surprisingly, all heaven became angry and eventually the wrath exploded. Atlantis was rent by earthquakes. Volcanoes erupted, and the ocean poured in. This land, which had once been so civilized, was utterly destroyed – with the exception of those distant outposts in Brazil.

When Fawcett put together the complicated jigsaw puzzle, compounded of the tales Indians told him, he decided that the location of this lost civilization must lie somewhere to the north of the Amazon – probably in a wild and dangerous part of Brazil known as the Mato Grosso. He called it simply 'Z'. Once he had come to this conclusion everything else became unimportant. Somehow, no matter what it cost, he had to find Z.

The outbreak of World War I interrupted his plans. By 1920, however, he was back in South America and setting off on another expedition. It was not a success. He preferred to travel with as little equipment as possible and with only a very few companions. Some explorers went into the jungle with a long train of friends and servants and goodness knows what else. That was not Fawcett's way. He believed that if food became scarce, the fewer mouths there were to feed, which was all the better. The trouble was that his impatience and his energy were such that nobody could keep up with him. Before the 1920 trip had gone very far his fellow travellers had run out of energy and his horse had died. He buried the animal in a jungle clearing he called Dead Horse Camp. Then, reluctantly, he turned back.

In 1925 he set off once more. This time he was accompanied by his son, Jack Fawcett, and by a young friend named Raleigh Rimmell. He was full of optimism about the venture. He warned his wife that he might not return until 1927, but when he came back his discoveries would astonish the world. Z had never seemed to be so near, and yet, as he knew very well, to reach it involved travelling through some very dangerous country.

The hazards came in many different forms. There were reptiles and wild animals, disease, shortages of food and water, and the Indians who might resent the intrusion of white men into their primitive world. Fawcett had always got on well with these people. He treated them with kindness and understanding and they invariably repaid him. But this could not be relied upon. A time might come when, instead of providing the help he expected, they would react with hostility.

Fawcett, his two companions, a few servants, eight mules and a small number of horses set off on their journey. Their only armament was a ·22 rifle for shooting game. They checked in at the northernmost military outpost – a collection of rundown buildings on top of a small hill surrounded by barbed wire and some dejected-looking palm trees. Then they moved on to Dead Horse Camp. At this point Fawcett decided to send back the servants and the horses. Raleigh Rimmell was now suffering from a sore foot and was obviously having difficulty in keeping up. Might it not be best if he, too, returned ? The young man refused. Somehow he would struggle on. His foot must eventually get better.

At Dead Horse Camp Fawcett wrote a letter to his wife. It must be taken, he said, to Herr Ahrens the German Consul at Cuiaba (the capital of the Mato Grosso state). Despite the fact that they were obviously being plagued by insects, and they had all been badly bitten, he seemed to be in excellent spirits. The letter ended with the words, 'You need have no fear of any failure . . .' Nevertheless, in an accompanying note to Ahrens, he wrote, 'It must be understood that it is, on the face of it, a highly dangerous undertaking.' It was

indeed. They were heading for the lands bordering the Xingu River. As a local saying had it, 'From the Xingu country no one ever comes back.' When, three years later, another expedition set off in this direction, it was referred to as 'The Suicide Club'.

'*You need have no fear of any failure.*' Those were the last words that Colonel Percy Harrison Fawcett ever wrote. From the moment the three white men left Dead Horse Camp, they vanished. Two years went by without anybody becoming unreasonably anxious. Fawcett had, after all, expected to be away for a long time. When three years had passed, however, people became worried. The British Ambassador at Rio de Janeiro received a telegram from the Royal Geographical Society in London. Would His Excellency ask the Brazilian Government whether they had received any news? His Excellency asked, and the Government said 'No'.

In New York an American naval officer named Commander George Dyott prepared to go in search of the missing men. As he soon discovered, it was going to be abominably difficult. One of the colonel's habits was to conceal his tracks. For example, he had even given misleading information about the location of Dead Horse Camp. It was situated approximately 14° south of the Equator, whereas he gave the position as 11°43' south. It is inconceivable that he could have been mistaken – it must have been deliberate.

Prospectors who went into the unknown were apt to obscure traces of their movements for businesslike reasons. If they discovered gold they wished to keep it to themselves. On the other hand, Fawcett was interested in wealth only as a means of finding Z. When he carefully rubbed out clues along the route his purpose was much

more high-minded. He was ready enough to surrender
his own life; he was not prepared to risk that of a search
party.

At about this time, far away in England, the Countess
of Westmorland found herself involved in the quest for
Fawcett. She was staying with some friends, among
whom was a clairvoyant. One evening, when they were
grouped around the crystal ball, a gentleman produced
a small scrap of paper. 'Does this have anything to say ?'
he asked. The clairvoyant asked them to leave the room.
When some minutes later they returned they found her
very distressed. At first, she said, she had seen a mass of
faces. They were all black and they looked very fierce.
Then the picture had changed and she was regarding a
lot of trees – it seemed to be a dense forest. As she peered
closer she could see a man lying on the ground. He
appeared to be dead. Presently another man came into
the picture. He was hacking his way through the
undergrowth and, at the same time, supporting a friend.
They had long hair and beards and their clothes were in
rags. To judge by their faces they seemed to be
half-starved – indeed, the friend was obviously on the
point of death. Now the natives were back again,
brandishing their spears and blowpipes: then suddenly
everything dissolved into a swirling pattern of blood.

Where had that scrap of paper come from ? The
gentleman explained that it had been torn off Colonel
Fawcett's last letter.

It was the first of many transmissions from the world
beyond concerning Fawcett. Even Commander Dyott
was treated to a report from a lady who, it was said, went
into trances. According to her story, the Colonel and his
son were prisoners of the Indians. She made no mention

of Raleigh Rimmell, and her testimony was not to be relied upon. They were, she said, living on the lower Xingi beside a river named the I-ti. There was no such thing. I-ti was the Indians' name for the sun.

But, despite Fawcett's obsession with secrecy, there were some clues. Beyond Dead Horse Camp Dyott came across marks in the shape of Ys carved in the trunks of trees. To leave behind such explicit pointers was not characteristic of the colonel, but how else could they be explained? There was also the evidence of a servant named Bernadino who had gone some distance beyond Dead Horse Camp with Fawcett. He escorted Dyott and his men to a river where, he said, Fawcett had helped himself to a pair of Indian canoes. They belonged to a tribe named the Anauqua; not surprisingly, the chief – a character named Aloique – was angry about this. Shortly after hearing the story Dyott met Aloique. He disliked the man immediately.

In Aloique's hut, however, the American discovered even more positive evidence that Fawcett and his two companions had passed this way. The chief's small son was wearing a piece of string with a metal tag on it round his neck. The tag bore the words 'W.S. Silver and Company, King William House, Eastcheap, London'. They were the makers of a small metal trunk that had definitely belonged to Fawcett. It was now lying in a corner of the hut.

According to the explorer's son, Brian Fawcett, this evidence was misleading. In his book, *Exploration Fawcett*, he explains that the trunk 'was one discarded by [my father] in 1920'. Nevertheless, Aloique insisted that it had been brought to him by a white man accompanied by two others, one of whom was lame.

When one remembers Rimmell's injured foot, the description seems remarkably fitting. In Dyott's mind there was no doubt that the chief had murdered the three men. By sign language, however, Aloique said that they had been ambushed by natives of another tribe five days after leaving his village.

The mystery was a little closer to being solved, though not very much. Meanwhile messages continued to come in from the great beyond until it seemed that every clairvoyant in the world was tuned into the Fawcett waveband. Most of them insisted that the three explorers were dead. However, in 1932, more encouraging news reached London, and this owed nothing to the spirit voices.

A Swiss trapper named Stefan Rattin had arrived in São Paulo with a most strange story. If he was to be believed, he and two friends had been washing their clothes in a stream one evening when a party of Indians surprised them. They were taken back to the camp where the chief offered them a potent local drink called xixa. As they sat drinking Rattin noticed an elderly white man some yards away. He had a long white beard and whitish-yellow hair. When they saw Rattin looking at the man, his hosts became suspicious. They were obviously unwilling for any communication to pass between the two of them.

Gradually the xixa began to take effect. The Indians became drunk, and then they fell asleep. Rattin seized the opportunity and went over to the white man. Before he could speak the man asked, 'Are you English ?' 'No – Swiss.' Strangely enough, although they both spoke Spanish fluently, it did not occur to either of them to use it. Instead, despite the fact that Rattin spoke it very badly, they struggled to exchange information in English.

The old man said he was a colonel in the British Army. When he got back to civilization Rattin should contact the nearest British consul and deliver a message. It was to be sent on to somebody named Paget. It was important that Paget should know that he was being held captive. Was that clear? Rattin nodded. The old man explained that his son was asleep in one of the huts but he made no mention of Rimmell. After that he broke down and cried.

Before they parted Rattin noticed that the 'English colonel' had cuts on the backs of his hands and he gave him some iodine. Next morning, however, it was found by the Indians – who snatched it away, and used it to paint designs on their naked bodies. For the time being there was nothing more to be done. The trapper and his two friends managed to depart without opposition.

Rattin now made his way to São Paulo where he was interviewed by General Candido da Silva Rondon, the head of the Brazilian Indian Commission and an authority on the country's interior. The General was sceptical. Why had they not spoken Spanish? Who was this man Paget? There'd been a diplomat named Sir Ralph Paget, who had been Ambassador at Rio during 1919 and 1920. Or was he referring to Major John Byng Paget, who had financed Fawcett's last expedition? Rattin hadn't the slightest idea.

The Brazilian official clearly suspected that Rattin was lying. But why? The trip to São Paulo had been a long one. It seemed pointless to take so much trouble simply to unload a lot of untruths. Had he anything to gain by it? Nothing! And then there were the details – such as the matter of iodine. It was unlikely that such an unimaginative character as Rattin would have made them up. He must surely have met a captive white man – the only question was: had he encountered Colonel Fawcett?

Rattin believed he had. As he explained, it was not unusual for the Indians to hold white men as hostages; some regarded them as mascots, others used them as servants. They were well treated unless they attempted to escape. Those who did were immediately recaptured and put to death. It was quite possible that Fawcett and his son were in this situation. So far as Rimmell was concerned, the young man might have died.

As he told people, Rattin was sure he could find his way back to the Indian camp. One day he announced that, since nobody else was willing, he intended to go on his own. He turned his back on São Paulo and set off for the jungle. It was the last that anyone saw or heard of him.

The years passed. By 1950 an organization named the Central Brazil Foundation had been established. The two brothers in charge of it, Orlando and Claudio Villas Boas, had won the Indians' trust. Orlando, indeed, had spent a year living with the Kalapolo tribe. During this period he became convinced that they had murdered Fawcett. It took a lot of time; but at last he persuaded them to confess. He even talked to the three men who admitted they had done the deed. Fawcett had, it seemed, disgraced himself by striking one of the Indians. It concerned a duck the Colonel had shot. When he saw a tribesman about to grab it he hit him across the face. Since such an action was wholly out of character, it was hard to believe. Could one, then, also credit the assertion that he had refused to present the Kalapolo tribe with beads and other gifts? According to the Indians, this had angered them so much that the Colonel and his two companions were clubbed to death. Their bodies were thrown into a lake.

When the chief heard about it he insisted that the corpses must be retrieved and properly buried. Now that the truth was out the bones were dug up and brought to England. At Claridges Hotel in London, they were handed over to the explorer's family, who asked the Royal Anthropological Institute to examine them.

When the report was produced it announced that the skeleton was all that remained of a man 1·70 *metres* high. Fawcett, you may remember, was 1·87 metres – his son and Raleigh Rimmell were both even taller. Nor were the teeth those of Percy Harrison Fawcett. Orlando Villas Boas may have discovered some of the truth; he certainly did not find the long-missing Colonel. But why, if the account was made up by the Indians, should an entire tribe confess to a murder that had never been committed ?

Throughout his adult life Colonel Fawcett was intrigued by puzzles. His death was the greatest puzzle of them all.

10 Journey into Nowhere

If money meant anything it should have been one of the most successful expeditions ever mounted. The Government of Victoria in Australia had contributed £12,000 towards the cost. In 1860 that was a fortune. But money alone is not enough to achieve the crossing of a continent. The sorry truth is that Robert O'Hara Burke was not the best of leaders. He was impatient, impulsive and a careless organizer.

The object was to cross Australia from south to north: from the lush plains on the edge of the Bass Strait to the unknown shores of the Gulf of Carpentaria. Once a route had been discovered it would be possible to erect a telegraph line – and for settlers to establish themselves. But it was obviously not going to be easy. In 1848 an explorer named Ludwig Leichardt had attempted it. He had set off into the interior – and was never seen again.

You might say that the present expedition was a race. At about the time Burke was making his plans an explorer named John MacDouall Stuart was working on a similar project. He was hoping to win a £10,000 prize offered by the state of South Australia for the first man to make the journey. Victoria, South Australia – each state wanted to become the rightful owner of land that had never been visited by white men before.

Robert Burke was a 40-year-old Irishman from Galway. He had served in the Belgian and Austro-Hungarian armies; now he was a police inspector at

Melbourne. His surveyor, who was also second-in-command of the expedition, was a younger man named William John Wills. He had studied as a medical student. In 1860, aged 27, he was employed at the meteorological office in Melbourne. He was gentle, whilst Burke was rough; thoughtful, whilst his leader acted on the spur of the moment. There must have been times when the two men were on the verge of quarrelling – but Wills, the peacemaker, prevented explosions.

They knew that, somewhere in between the south and north coasts, there was a great desert. Camels seemed to be a more sensible means of transportation than horses and a number were imported from India. A man named Landells was put in charge of them. William Brahne was appointed foreman: among the other fourteen travellers two men – John King and George Grey – were to play particularly important roles in the story. They were both friends of Burke.

On 20 August 1860 the cavalcade set out from Melbourne. It seemed as if the entire city had turned out to wish them good luck. Burke, an impressive figure with his proud bearing and his thick black beard, responded to the cheers with a wave of his hand. Did he realize the dangers of his task, the innumerable difficulties that lay between a triumphant departure and an even more glorious return? Nothing in his self-confident manner suggested it.

But what could go wrong? They had sufficient camels, a few horses, masses of stores and none of the men was wanting in courage. Unfortunately they lacked a quality that was of paramount importance: experience. None of them had ever been on this kind of expedition before.

Before they had gone very far Burke made two

mistakes. The first was to divide the expedition into two: a main party and an advance party. The former was put under the command of a man named Wright. Burke intended to hurry on ahead with seven men, including Wills, King and Grey. Wright was to rejoin them at a point named Cooper's Creek. A range of mountains and a desert now lay between the advance guard and the bulk of their supplies.

Either Wright was the wrong man for the job or else his orders were vague. He was left behind in a village named Menindie on the Darling River and there he remained for three months. If Burke's fault was impatience (he was too eager to press on ahead) Wright's was the opposite. He seemed quite happy to remain in this pleasant spot beside the river, if need be, for ever.

The other mistake depleted the complement of camels. Burke was a difficult man to get on with. Landells had done something to make him angry. The Irishman erupted and they were soon engaged in a furious row. Such outbursts may have been unremarkable in the Austro-Hungarian army but it was not the way to handle men such as these. Landells was fed up. Taking some of the animals with him he turned back. King was put in charge of the remaining beasts.

Burke and his advance guard reached Cooper's Creek on 11 November 1860. They established a small camp and sat down to wait for Wright and the main party. One day followed another and still there were no signs of them. Burke became more and more impatient; after five weeks he could stand it no longer. Never mind about the others! Brahne would remain at Cooper's Creek with three men. He would take Wills, King and Grey with him and hurry on northwards. If they did not return within three months Brahne should return to Melbourne.

On 16 December they departed from Cooper's Creek with six camels, one horse, and three months' supply of food. On 20 December they arrived at a large lagoon where there was plenty of wildfowl to eke out the rations. What was more, the banks were populated by aborigines. Some explorers had found the natives hostile but these dark-skinned men and women were friendly. In the tradition of explorers, Burke and his men had brought supplies of beads, nails and, in this instance, matches. Their new friends were happy to do business. They were delighted with the gifts and gave the white men fresh food in return. The diet had been somewhat monotonous; now, with wild duck and fish on the menu, meals were something to be enjoyed.

Less than a month later, on 7 January, they crossed the Tropic of Capricorn. The journey so far had been good. Burke had expected problems due to lack of water. In fact, there had been ample supplies. But now the situation changed – though not as Burke had expected. Instead of too little water, he found too *much* of it. It was certainly very bad luck: there had been exceptionally heavy rainfall in northern Australia that year. After crossing the tropic, the dry landscape, adorned with palm trees and the picturesque flights of cockatoos, suddenly melted into bog. For miles and miles, and then more miles, Burke and his companions squelched through deep mud.

Their progress was now very much slower. Eventually, on 3 February, Burke's impatience could stand it no longer. King and Grey were to remain behind. Taking with them a horse and three days' provisions, he and

Wills would make the last leg of the journey on their own.

On 11 February they reached a point that, according to their calculations, should have been on the north coast. But, instead of seeing the gleaming waters of the Gulf of Carpentaria, they were rewarded with nothing more than a dismal view of scrub and swampland stretching out ahead. It was impossible to wade through it; the only thing was to turn back. Still, they had crossed the continent. That, surely, was enough. Somewhere in front lay the sea – if only they had been able to set eyes on it.

With bits and pieces of his expedition now littered across half Australia, with heavy rain making the going extremely difficult, and with Burke urging the advance guard to almost impossible feats of endurance, it was, perhaps, a miracle that they had ever reached the north coast. But every man had his limits. Would they be able to return?

By early March Grey was complaining about feeling unwell. On the 3rd of that month Burke himself became sick. It was his own fault. He had come across a giant snake, 2·54 metres long. Since food was running short he killed it – and ate the flesh. Before very long he suffered a severe attack of dysentery.

Burke had remarkable powers of recovery; it was as if he overcame illness by sheer willpower. Charles Grey was less robust. He continued to grumble about his health – sometimes, he experienced acute pain. Or so he said; the others doubted it. They accused him of shamming. On one occasion, when he was suspected of stealing rations, Burke (to quote Wills) gave him 'a good thrashing'. Poor Grey – in fact, he was very sick indeed;

and, on 17 April, he died. Four of the six camels were also dead, and the only remaining food was half a kilogram of dried meat.

Still, there was no cause for alarm. They were only a comparatively short distance from Cooper's Creek. As Burke told his companions, Brahne and his men would be waiting for them. With a bit of luck Wright would also be there with the main party. Their troubles were over. The rest of the return trip would be safely, even comfortably, accomplished.

Unfortunately Burke had forgotten something. He had told Brahne to pull out if they did not return within twelve weeks. They had now been away from Cooper's Creek for four months. Unless Brahne had ignored his instructions the depot would be deserted.

In fact, the foreman did ignore his orders. He remained at Cooper's Creek for four months. By one of those wretched accidents of fate he departed on the very morning that Burke and his surviving two companions arrived. They had missed each other by only an hour or so.

Yes, Cooper's Creek was deserted. It was a bitter disappointment. Burke's first impulse was to move on at once in an attempt to catch up with the others. It was obviously impossible. As William Wills noted in his diary, after four months of privation 'our legs are almost paralysed, so that each of us finds it a most trying task to walk a few yards'. Their animals were also exhausted, whilst Brahne's were fresh after a long rest. They could not hope to catch up; any attempt to overtake the departed men would be futile and dangerous.

One of the trio was wandering disconsolately around the camp-site when he noticed a piece of paper nailed

to a tree. On it was written, 'DIG 3 ft NW'. They dug. Concealed in a small hole they came across a note from Brahne explaining his actions, and a supply of rations. That night they ate porridge and sugar for supper. Afterwards they felt better. Burke's spirits, especially, had recovered. He was now full of plans – all of which added up to making the return trip by another route. Instead of going back to Melbourne, they would head for Adelaide.

The others argued with him. Surely it would be best to travel by the way they knew? To go off into unexplored country would be crazy. But Burke was adamant. Next morning they moved off into the wilderness.

The following two months were a nightmare. One by one they killed off the camels for food – cutting the flesh off their bones and drying it – until only a beast named Rajah remained. With every step they seemed to become weaker. Unaccountably, Burke decided that essential stores – such as sugar and ginger, tea and cocoa – must be thrown away. He kept on explaining that they should carry only what was absolutely essential. But he seemed to be confused about what this meant. Food, surely, was necessary?

By 6 May their clothing was in rags and their boots were falling to pieces. On the following morning Rajah was unable to get up. The unhappy animal was shot; its dried flesh was now their only food. They were alone in the wilderness with no animals to assist them – and, though Burke did not seem to realize it, lost.

But in this God-forsaken land, with its huge tracts of emptiness, there were people. What was more, they were friendly. During the second week of June they stumbled on a native village. They ate the last of Rajah's flesh and the aborigines taught them to make a kind of flour from the seeds of a plant named nardoo ('it looks like clover). Wills was now too weak to walk. King was in a sorry condition, and even Burke was showing signs of severe strain. On 21 June, Wills noted in his diary,

'Unless relief comes in some form or another, I cannot possibly last more than a fortnight.' Eight days later he wrote, 'Nothing now but the greatest good luck can save us; and as for myself, I may live four or five days, if the weather continues warm.'

Wills knew what he was writing about; he had, after all, been a medical student. Only a miracle could save him, and there was no likelihood of one occurring. But need they all die? Burke decided that his ailing second-in-command must be left behind. He and King would move on in an attempt to find some more aborigines. It was their only hope. Wills agreed. Yes – it was the best thing to do.

If only they had known it, they had been within yards of the much desired miracle on 8 May. Brahne had set off from Cooper's Creek with an uneasy conscience. He had remained there four weeks longer than Burke had instructed. By that time, he had assumed the advance party had either returned by a different route – through Queensland – or else they had perished in the desert. Nevertheless, he was not happy. Eventually, after days of arguing with himself, he decided to return to the creek.

At that time Burke, Wills and King were going round in circles. They, too, came to a point not far from the creek – at the very moment when Brahne and his men were approaching it from another direction. But they never saw them. When Brahne arrived he found no message for him. The wind and the rain had demolished all footprints, and it did not occur to him to see whether the buried stores had been broached. He turned away, never realizing that the others were so close.

Burke's health was now very bad. He complained of fierce pains in his back and in his legs. At last he could go no farther. He threw away his small bundle of possessions, and lay down. That evening he ate a crow that King had shot and some powdered nardoo. Afterwards, he handed King his watch and his pocket book. Far from doing him good, the food seemed to have worsened his condition. He clasped his pistol in his right hand and said to his companion, 'I hope that you will remain with me till I am quite dead.' During the night he spoke little. At eight o'clock on the following morning he died.

King was now on his own and desperately lonely. For want of any better idea he decided to go back and see whether Wills was still alive. It was a hopeless plan; he was far too weak and it was unreasonable to hope that Wills *would* have survived. But King was fortunate. At some point he came across a tribe of natives. At first they tried to turn him away, but King was desperate. Somehow he managed to communicate with them; somehow he managed to explain his plight. If only they'd accept him as one of them . . . The aborigines relented. For the next three months he lived with them, existing on a diet of nardoo, fish and 'fat rats'.

With no news of the explorers reaching Melbourne it was obvious that something had gone badly wrong. They should be back by now. Even allowing for difficulties produced by the weather they were long overdue. Four expeditions went off in search of them. On 18 September one of them, led by Alfred Howitt, came across King. Howitt described him as 'of a melancholy appearance – wasted to a straw and hardly to be distinguished as a civilized being but by the remnants of clothes upon him'.

But he was alive – which was more than could be said of the others.

In January 1863 the body of Burke was brought back to Melbourne. On the 22nd of the month his funeral took place. His remains were carried in a hearse six metres long – with The Royal coat of arms mounted on the front. The procession of mourners was estimated as being 0·8 kilometres long and thousands of people lined the route. A military band played the Dead March: just as his departure for the Gulf of Carpentaria, so was Robert O'Hara Burke's last journey made in triumph. It was a pity he couldn't see it.

Burke's rival, Stuart, had turned back when he reached a point about midway across the continent. The telegraph line and the colonization of the Gulf of Carpentaria would have to wait. If anybody doubted the difficulties of getting there by land, he had only to talk to John King.

Richard Garrett
Great Sea Mysteries 40p

A collection of fascinating stories of great oceans and strange ships, master-spies and mutineers, sabotage and the supernatural, the heroism of young Grace Darling, and the never-ending mystery of the *Mary Celeste* . . .

Marie Herbert
Great Polar Adventures 40p

Eleven thrilling stories of men who risked their lives to get to the ends of the earth. The quest for the Poles started as early as Elizabethan times but they have only been properly explored in the last few years. Wallie Herbert's story is included in this collection and you can plot the routes on the maps he has drawn.

John Gilbert
Pirates and Buccaneers 40p

Read the true stories of twenty-four of the infamous pirates who have made history with their dash and lawlessness. Such ruthless and bloodthirsty captures can never cease to shock and fascinate.

You can buy these and other Piccolo Books from booksellers and newsagents; or direct from the following address:
Pan Books, Sales Office, Cavaye Place, London SW10 9PG
Send purchase price plus 20p for the first book and 10p for each additional book, to allow for postage and packing
Prices quoted are applicable in the UK

While every effort is made to keep prices low, it is sometimes necessary to increase prices at short notice. Pan Books reserve the right to show on covers and charge new retail prices which may differ from those advertised in the text or elsewhere.